Curtis

SOME AMERICAN PEOPLE

ERSKINE CALDWELL

SOME AMERICAN PEOPLE

NEW YORK
ROBERT M. McBRIDE & COMPANY

SOME AMERICAN PEOPLE

COPYRIGHT, 1935
BY ERSKINE CALDWELL

PRINTED IN THE UNITED STATES
OF AMERICA

FIRST EDITION

CONTENTS

I.

ADVERTISEMENT

ADVERTISEMENT

Americans with means of traveling do not know how to travel. They have to be enticed with such slogans as "See America First." They must be convinced that travel is fashionable or, anyway, educational. And finally, after they have been persuaded to give up their radios and bridge partners for a few days or weeks, they must be made to believe that the trip is worth the time and money spent. And then, once ready to go, traveling Americans are off like a whirlwind, confusing travel with sheer motion. Even then the boredom of constantly changing scenery and faces drives them to magazines and cards, where the relativity of time is reduced to their own level.

3

There are no memorials, vistas, or landmarks anywhere between the Atlantic and Pacific worthy of going fifty miles to see. Once seen, these Grand Views are relegated to the catalogue merely used to summon up topics for small talk. They are only the lures, after all, of commercial intercourse.

What is worth traveling thousands of miles to see and know are people and their activity. Each geographical division, practically each state, in America has its own peculiar and arresting background. The majesty of nature is a trivial sight when it is not viewed in relation to man and his activity. Merely to see things is not enough; only the understanding of man's activity is satisfying.

The sections that follow give account of a small amount of travel done during a year's time, from May 1934 to May 1935, in the United States. No descriptions of monuments, canyon sunsets, waterfalls, or mountain glaciers are to be found therein. What is described is some of the influence of nature upon man, and a portion of the combat between man and man.

The first section, called "Cross-Country," is a

partial account of a journey from the West Coast
to the Atlantic, covering more than five thousand miles. It would be an absurd pretension to
imply that one person saw and experienced all
that it is possible to see and experience during
such a trip. What is lacking in the account is
suggested by the shortness of the account.

During such a trip the contact with people is
the one and all-important matter. To make a
dash by automobile of five or six hundred miles
a day, to arrive at night at a metropolitan hotel
only to enquire for the home newspapers, and
to start out again the next morning by asking
how far it is to home, is to make a trip of incon-
sequential value. Travelers who go to the
expense of transporting themselves from Massachusetts to Arizona only to complain habitually
for three weeks about the absence of seafood on
the menu would have had a much better time if
they had stayed at home and gone to the movies
every night. There is nothing to be gained in
travel if the traveler is not prepared to accept,
or capable of experiencing, a change of habits,
thought, and diet. In attempting to impose his

own questionable idiosyncrasies upon others, he
not only disgusts those with whom he comes in
contact, but has a dismal time of it himself. The
most flagrant offenders are those Americans with
ample means to travel: in their ostentatious be-
havior they act like fish out of the water.

The middle section is called "Detroit." This
is a chapter about the automobile workers in
the Michigan city. Instead of being a running,
rambling account of places and people in many
states, it is confined to those men and women in
Detroit who build the American automobile.
Like workers confined to any specialized industry, they are the victims of a condition. Because
the specialized industry, in its labor, is a non-
individualistic enterprise, the worker lives ac-
cording to his ability to coöperate with his fellow workers. In the automobile industry the
open-shop policy has brought about a straggling,
disorganized condition of labor. It is one of the
clearest examples of industrial slavery. Some
automobile manufacturers permit the labor
union to function in their plants; some install
their own company unions, over which the

worker has practically no control; and some
plants have rigorously outlawed the right of
labor to bargain collectively, either through
company unions or national labor unions. As a
result, the automobile worker is cut off from any
means of giving voice to dissatisfaction with the
manufacturer's autocratic rule.

The final section is called "Southern Tenant
Farmers." This is an account of people in the
cotton states, living under decivilized conditions. Much has been written about the Southern
Negro and the Southern White, but much of the
matter has been a garbled mixture of romance
and mis-statement. The traveler who visits the
cotton states should follow his own nose, rather
than follow a set or planned itinerary, because
once there, he will discover paths still undis-
covered. Here, on his own for several weeks or
months, he will come close to humanity.

The cotton states extend from the Atlantic,
broad-beamed from North Carolina and South
Carolina, to Texas. They constitute an empire, a
newly formed nation, in themselves. The cus-
toms, language, thought, clothing, food, and

appearances set the cotton states apart. The combination of climate and cotton has formed—simultaneously with the integration of America, but belatedly recognized—a nation within a nation. These cotton states have produced a national peon, an undernourished, undereducated, underpaid laborer, who is now at last fighting to regain equal rights with his countrymen. He is the Southern tenant farmer.

There are more than two-score states, there are hundreds of cities, and there are thousands of miles of wayside, and each has its own specialized character. Each of them, if viewed from the point of view of its people, has a different story to tell. By visiting sections of the country, such as the cotton states, the Northwest, and tight, industrialized New England, the stories of its people will be found in ever changing versions. Such cities as Detroit, Scranton, Salt Lake City, Omaha, Birmingham, and Worcester have stories of coal, cloth, wheat, packing, and steel to tell to anyone who wishes to hear.

None of these chapters pretends to be an exhaustive study. Neither do they intend to imply, collectively, that they offer a surprise package of plumed panaceas. Their sole purpose is to show, by a few examples, what can be seen and experienced in America today and tomorrow. The traveler is given this promise, and warning.

Travel should not be confused with sightseeing and touring, the latter two being pastimes of idle wealth. In its true meaning, a traveler is a stranger who gains a sympathetic understanding with the people he encounters. It is not necessary for the traveler to have wealth; the most satisfactory travel is sometimes done by means of foot and freight car. Those who stay at home, either because of inclination or because of ignorance, and those who travel like a whirlwind are both to be pitied: they do not know what they are missing.

II.

CROSS-COUNTRY

CHAPTER I.

ON THE RANGE

IN CENTRAL Oregon, on the eastern slope of the Cascade Mountains, the shriveled grass is lying on the range like scraps of steel shavings. A gust of hot wind sweeps down to earth, and with your ear to the ground you hear a sound like somebody kicking rusty springs through the wiry brown grass.

Over on a hillside the wind is making ripples on the dusty contour of the range; down below, in the pocket of a dry stream bed, the wind is carving precise images on the drifted sand.

The rainfall has been normal; the trouble is that normal is not enough. Fifteen inches a year will never be enough even to settle the dust, whether it be in Oregon or Arizona or Colorado.

13

At ten o'clock in the morning all the stores in the town of Madras that were going to open, had opened. Half of them have been vacant and boarded shut for nearly a year; the hardware merchant and the drygoods merchant couldn't get by on just taking in each other's washing.

A man has come up from somewhere and sits down on the step of a boarded-up store building. Overhead on the second-story false front —the dashboard—the few remaining flakes of paint inform you that clothing for the family was sold there once. The man on the step is wearing faded blue denim pants, a colorless, soiled white shirt, and dusty brogans. It has been two months since he last had a haircut.

You walk a block in Madras, in any direction, and you are on the open range. As far as the eye can see, the rolling earth extends mile after mile towards an infinite horizon. The brown sod is frequently broken by squares and ovals of dusty, drifting fields. They look as if they might be tumbled-over tombstones, once erected to the faded hope of dry-farming.

Back from the range, you are still on the range, in Madras. The man on the step has not moved in an hour's time. He still sits looking out into the deserted street. Perhaps his hair is a little longer, perhaps not; but you can't help thinking that it hangs a little lower around his neck.

You raise a hand in greeting, but receive no response. You have elected to come to Madras, and you must accept the permeating silence of the range.

Behind the man, on the dusty windows, the lettering says it is Johnson's Store. Wiping away some of the accumulated dust, you press your face against the glass, shading your eyes with your hands, and try to see inside. The interior of the place has the appearance of the variety store at home the morning after Christmas. Empty boxes, scraps of paper, and bare shelves show that it has been stripped clean of its wares.

You take a seat on the step beside the man. "Who owns this store?"

The man on the step spits into the street. "If you mean the four walls, I reckon the bank does."

"Who owned it before the bank took it over?"

"I used to think I did."

You settle yourself on the step beside Johnson, spit into the street, and fall into his silence for a while. Two or three automobiles rumble past. It is nearing the noon hour.

You begin wondering presently, aloud, if there is much activity on the range around Madras since the Government shipped the cattle out.

"How can there be?" Johnson says. "A man would be a fool to ride out and go through the motions of herding cows, when there ain't a cow in sight. Now, wouldn't he?"

"That's right. But people have got to do something."

"Not these people," Johnson says. "Not here."

You get up and look at your watch. It is a long drive to the Columbia River. "Everybody can't live on the Government," you suggest. "Probably a lot of ranchers will get together some herds in the spring."

"Maybe," Johnson replies. "But by spring I don't look for more than a handful of folks around here. People are going to follow the cows. That's what brought me here, and I reckon I'm pretty much like everybody else."

"That sounds like good reasoning," you say, "because cattle-raising built up most of this part of the country. But a lot of people have got out of the habit of following the cows—they think they can raise wheat on ten to fifteen inches of rainfall."

Johnson chuckles to himself. "That wheat-raising business wasn't the people's fault. These scientific fellows who do their wheat farming in an office building with a stenographer sitting on their laps brought about all that dry-farming foolishness. Cows wasn't good enough for them. If they had come out and lived on the range, they'd have learned what the range's good for."

When you are getting ready to leave, Johnson calls you back to the step for a moment. "If you ever run across any of those scientific dry-farmers, tell them that about the most foolish thing a man can do is to break up the sod on a short-grass range. If they want to learn something, tell them that any country that grows rabbits taller than the buffalo grass is a cow country, and where the grass grows taller than the rabbits, that's a wheat country."

CHAPTER II.

ROUTE U. S. 10

THE Peppy Filling Station, located in suburban Spokane on the Coeur d'Alene highway, is doing more business than it ever did before. In 1932 it was open sixteen hours a day, and the owners were satisfied with the profit it made; in 1933 business was so good that the station was operated twenty-four hours a day; in 1934 the owners hired an extra man for the night shift, and began to wonder why so many Dakota automobiles were going West.

It would have been difficult in the spring of that year to locate in all America three hundred thousand motor vehicles registered in the two Dakotas. And yet the Peppy boys say more Dakota cars, westbound, stop and buy gasoline and oil than cars from any other state in the

Union, with the exception of Washington and Idaho.

Long before the middle of the summer they found out why they were selling gasoline to so many Dakota motorists. The North Dakotans and the South Dakotans were telling the Peppy boys things they never knew before. The arid mid-continent was reclaiming the land whose sod men had broken in an attempt to dry-farm. Wheat was a mighty good Dakota product, as long as it was raised on the prairie; but when the sod on the hills and slopes was turned twelve inches under, it ceased to be dry-farming and became suicide. Gulley-washing rains were turning the hills and slopes into pipestones and Badlands faster than the surveyors could plot their maps. There was not enough sodded prairie left in some counties to supply grazing grounds for cattle and sheep. The winter snows, the backbone of dry-farming, were running off into the Badland gulches and canyons instead of soaking into the sod for summer wheat and grass.

The Peppy boys wished to know where the

Dakotans were going, and why. The Dakotans themselves, on Route U. S. 10, were quick to answer: they were going to the western slope of the Cascades, because they had heard that there was always moisture there. For three years most of them had not had enough water for their stock, let alone enough to grow crops. They had heard that west of the Cascade Mountains the rainfall was above forty inches a year, every year; in North and South Dakota the normal rainfall has always been less than twenty inches, and for the past three years it has been fifty per cent below normal. Going from a land where three years of deficient moisture had withered life in plant and animal to a country where water drips from the skies in abundance—you can bet your life the Dakotans knew where they were going, and why!

The Peppy Filling Station is still selling tanksful of gasoline to the one-way travelers. Only one out of every five cars bearing North or South Dakota license plates has returned eastward yet, the Peppy boys estimate. There will be room for them all in western Oregon and Washington; but there will be even more room in the

Dakotas for those who go back and take steps to return the sod to the hills and slopes where it binds the dark mellow earth firmly and securely.

Families packed in sedans with all the household goods they are able to take with them speed westward past the Peppy boys day after day and all through the night. Not all of them stop to fill their tanks at the Peppy Filling Station, but all of them, from infant to feeble grandmother, speed along the Coeur d'Alene-Spokane highway with eyes fastened on the road ahead. It is a new country, almost a virgin country, to the Dakotans; it is rolling and green, and the trees and shrubs are mirages to prairie eyes; but it still is not over the Cascades.

The Peppy boys have a cash drawer full of hard round dollars that have been handed to them through the windows of Dakota sedans. There would be more, but every once in a while they pass one or two of them back again, hoping it will help complete the distance to the far side of the Cascades.

A North Dakota car passes, westerly; a Montana coupé, then two sedans in line from South

Dakota. Directly in the rear of the group a local truck grinds slowly forward, and then out from behind it suddenly emerges a dusty baggage-burdened sedan bearing North Dakota license plates. For a moment it looks as if it will speed up and overtake the cars ahead, but fifty feet away the driver slows down and turns into the grounds of the Peppy boys. The motor is shut off, the occupants begin climbing out the best they can, squeezing between suitcase and canvas bags filled with bedding.

"Welcome to Spokane!" one of the Peppy boys says.

"How far is it to Wenatchee?" one of the two elderly men inquires quickly.

"Going to Wenatchee?"

"Going to take a look at it," he replies, "but we're all fixed to go right on through to Puget Sound."

The Peppy boy cleans the windshield. "We've got a mighty fine country in this part of Washington," he says.

The North Dakotan squints at the rolling hills and, finally, at the sky. "When's the last time you had a rain?" he asks, glaring up at the cloudless blue sky.

"Well," the Peppy boy replies, "I don't believe I remember exactly, but it hasn't been—"

The North Dakotan hustles the family back into the sedan, slams the door, and starts the motor. Before the Peppy boy can hand him a highway map, the driver speeds out of the filling station yard and dives into the stream of traffic, westbound.

CHAPTER III.

A BADLAND TALE

THE Billings, Montana, autocamp owner was anxious to know if we had heard the story about the banker in a small town in the North Dakota Badlands. We told him we had been listening to Dakota drouth stories, North and South, ever since we had left the Pacific Coast; but, if his version was anything like the others, it would be a different story, and naturally we would like to hear it.

However, we had heard about the drouth in the Dakotas; what about the drouth in Montana?

"It's bad enough here," he said; "but it's been dry in this part of the country ever since the war."

Which war, we asked him; the World War, or the Civil War?

"The Indian War," he said. "That was 'way back yonder."

Anyway, we told him, you don't have to live in constant fear of the Indians these days, since there are barely enough of them left to sell beads to the tourists. Back in the days when the Indians raided the settlements, a man didn't have much time for thinking about drouths, what with fighting Indians and chasing stage-coach robbers day and night.

"No," the fellow said, "but pretty soon we'll have to start thinning out the Government agents, or there won't be enough room left in Billings for the cow hands when they come to town to do their spending. New loads of agents come in here from Washington or somewhere every day. First they come and buy up all the cattle; then after they've taken a man's living away from him, a new train-load comes in to hand out food and clothes; after they run out of people to feed and dress, another bunch hops off the train and begins handing out picks and shovels so the people will have something to occupy their time with. It's getting so in Montana these days that if you don't draw Government pay, you don't have any social standing at all."

We reminded him of the story he was going to tell us about the Badlands.

"Some people say it happened in South Dakota," he said, "but I know for a fact that it took place in North Dakota. Down south there there's Badlands, but there's Badlands in the north where they have bankers, too. I know for a fact that there's been bankers in North Dakota, because I've been there and seen them myself."

The story we had heard the most, we said, was about a man who ran a filling station. It was somewhere around the Black Hills, in South Dakota, and the fellow was first seen to be acting queerly one morning when he went out and began pumping gasoline into the imaginary tank of an imaginary automobile. He had not sold a drop of real gasoline to a real motor-car owner in three or four weeks, and the people—

"That's far enough," the autocamp owner

said; "that's not the genuine, real Dakota story. Over there in—"

Anyway, we insisted, people noticed the fellow going through the motions of filling up the gas tank on a car, and pretty soon another man, who used to run a filling station before the drouth, went out and began wiping the imaginary windshield of the imaginary car.

"To save my life I don't know how such tales get started these days," the man said. "Anybody can tell there's not a drop of truth in it from beginning to end. When I finish telling you about this banker in this little town in North Dakota, anybody would swear to the truth of it, because it's exactly the way the thing happened."

Before he went any further we promised the autocamp owner that we would believe his version just as much as we had believed any of the previous ones.

"This banker had lost his shirt in the drouth," he said. "He lost his bank, his house, and his car. He didn't have a penny to his name nowhere in the world. And, like everybody else who wasn't working for the Government, he spent his

time loafing around one of the stores in town.
There were plenty of others hanging around,
too; but he was the outstanding one, because before that he had been the man who owned all
the money in town, not to mention the biggest
house and the shiniest car.

"One morning one of these Government agents
happened to have a minute to spare, and he sat
down in front of a store to rest and cool off.
Just about that time the banker glanced at his
watch, got up from his seat, and walked out into
the street. He began to warm up, like a baseball
pitcher. He was throwing the ball to what might
have been a catcher, if there had been a catcher.
After warming up a few minutes, he motioned
to the batter that he was ready. The first ball
he threw over the plate was a called strike. The
second one was a ball, a little on the outside.
The banker threw down his glove, jumped up
and down on it half a dozen times, and started
arguing with the umpire for calling it a ball.
Pretty soon he listened to the third baseman,
and agreed to accept the umpire's decision. He
stepped back into his box, motioned the out-

fielders to come in a little closer for a left-handed batter. He threw the ball across, and the batter singled.

"The Government agent who had been watching the thing with his mouth hanging open, turned to one of the other loafers sitting beside him and asked how long the banker had been acting like that. The fellow told him for a couple of months—ever since the drouth got bad. The agent asked him if he didn't feel sorry for the banker. The fellow shook his head. 'No,' he said, 'I can't afford to do that, because the minute I started feeling sorry for him, I'd lose the grip I've got on myself and go out there and catch for him.' "

CHAPTER IV.

THE LAST ROUNDUP

THERE probably will never be in America another roundup as large as the mid-August cattle drive in western North Dakota in 1934. Ten thousand head of stock were driven out of the Badlands in two days' time and loaded for shipment at the Williston terminal.

Aside from being one of the largest drives, it was one of the quickest. For once the Federal Government was not hampered in its efforts by red tape. The emergency drive which ordinarily might have consumed ten days or two weeks, was accomplished in two days and nights. The grassless Badlands, the parched prairie of the Little Missouri River country had ten thousand hungry animals. Individual stockmen and ranchers were unable to cope with the emergency; it was only by means of the prompt and unified action of Federal agencies that the wholesale cattle relief plan was carried out.

In Williston at the end of the roundup, while the cowhands rested from the drive, another task almost as great was begun. Inspectors worked day and night slapping green paint on the ribs of grazing stock which were then loaded for shipment to Georgia and other southern states where pastures were greener. Slaughter stock was marked with the uniform U. S. brand, and loaded on cattle cars for shipment to the stockyards. During all that time veterinarians culled the herds. Stock that was too poor to stand shipment was killed on the spot and buried immediately.

Three years of drouth came to an end in mid-August as far as the cattle of the Badlands were concerned. Ranchers who had been buying hay at eighteen dollars a ton had reached the end of their rope; banks had long since stopped lending money to feed stock on a declining market; and the Federal Government had laid down

a policy of not making feed loans on anything
except breeding stock.

In July, with one final sweep, the Government had decided that the Badlands was un-
suited to cattle-raising; it had even gone so
far as to insinuate that it was unsuitable for
human habitation, which was going too far.
The Badlands were undoubtedly overpopulated
with cattle; but human beings have a way of
clinging to a country that best suits their needs
and desires.

Appraising and buying of stock began in July,
and shipments were to be spread over the following months. But an already critical situation
became an emergency. There was no water, no
feed; animals were dropping to the ground and
never rising again. By taking over the cattle,
the Government had become liable for their
keep; it was receiving messages advising it to
come and take care of the stock it had bought
and left unprovided for. It was then mid-August,
and there was only one course left open; there
had to be a last roundup.

Back in the wake of the drive, the ranchers

stood and looked at their bare lands. They had sold their means of livelihood; for, once the Government stepped in to take charge, it had decided that not even breeding stock would be left behind. The end of the little dogie in western North Dakota had come.

There were residents of the Slope country, that section of western North Dakota which extends one hundred and fifty miles east and west and two hundred miles north and south—otherwise known as the Badlands—who had not been cattle-owners. They were the workers, the cowhands, the small farmers, who were holding desperately to the last remnant of their homesteads —the settlers of 1899 who had received as a gift from the Federal Government four hundred and eighty acres of land; homestead, preëmption, and tree claim—and they were left stranded in a denuded country.

The Government's next step was to buy up as much of the land as it could. A million dollars was allocated for the purpose. Agents began the six months' task of interviewing the landowners, appraising the ranches, and offering six, eight, ten dollars an acre.

There was still another group of residents of the Badlands: there were men and women who owned no more than the clothes on their backs. They had nothing to sell; they were without cattle, land, or homes.

The Government was determined in its policy towards the Slope country, and so it offered to transport families to sustenance lands in Arkansas.

The Government could drive ten thousand head of cattle to the last roundup in two days, but it could not drive five thousand human beings to other states. If the Government is determined to strip the country, it may create a national park in the area; but the move is not likely, since its dealings now are with the people, not cattle.

Former cattle- and land-owners with Government checks in their pockets continue to head westward beyond the Cascades. But in the Badlands men and women and children will always live. It will become once more a pioneer country, where only the strong will be able to survive, and for that reason those who remain will be the more fortunate.

The last great roundup is over, the bones of the culls that fell by the wayside have been picked clean, and the painted canyons of the Badlands are unchanged.

Next spring the tide of travel will turn; a lot of people are coming back home.

CHAPTER V.

THE BARBER OF THE NORTHWEST

A NORTHERN PACIFIC freight train rolled in from the prairie, eighty-eight cars long, and ground to a screeching stop on the embankment above the baseball park. The visiting House of David team was beating the locals 7 to 5 in the seventh inning, but Bismarck was up with two men on, one out, and the lead-off man was planting a single in right field. A relief pitcher climbed out of the House of David dugout and began warming up on the sidelines. It looked pretty bad for the visitors.

The N.P. shook itself two or three times in quick succession, like a dog remembering its fleas, and a handful of hoboes clambered out of the gondolas and box cars and dropped to the ground. The sixty or seventy men and boys

37

who remained on the train would reach Fargo sometime that night.

Down in the dell the forty-cent fans were on their feet in grandstand and bleachers. Somebody had driven a long fly to center field for a sacrifice hit, and a runner scored.

A man dropped beside me on the edge of the embankment and began opening up a leather satchel.

"What's the score?" he asked, taking out some things and placing them in a neat row on the ground.

I pointed to the scoreboard down in the dell.

The fellow glanced up for the first time and squinted down into the playing field.

"Whiskers, eh?" he said, and spat to one side.

The bearded House of David team was making an easy out at first base, and coming in for their turn at bat. The score stood 7 to 6 in their favor now.

The fellow closed the satchel and placed it to one side. Picking up a whetstone with one hand, he selected with the other a pearl-handled razor from his collection of three. He began honing the blade.

"Barber?" he asked.

"Who? Me?" I said.

He nodded.

"No," I said.

He took a quick, close look at my face.

"I can give you a once-over in a couple of minutes," he offered.

I felt my face.

"I guess I can get by until tomorrow," I told him.

"O.K.," he said.

The fellow poured a little water from a tin bottle into a mug and began working up a lather. When it was ready, he set up a mirror and began applying it to his face.

"Are you a barber?" I asked him.

He stopped what he was doing and looked at me.

"Don't you know me?" he asked in surprise.

I shook my head.

"Haven't you ever traveled on the N.P.?"

I told him I never had.

"O.K.," he said, leaning forward to look into the mirror. "I'm Happy Flynn. I've been riding the N.P. for three years; everybody who rides the N.P. knows me. I'm the barber."

"On the freights?" I asked.

"Sure," Flynn said. "On the freights."

A big Negro swung off the refrigerator car behind us and stretched out on the embankment, with his pack under his head, to watch the baseball game in the dell.

The barber got up, halfway through shaving, and went over to where the Negro lay. They talked for a few minutes, and then he came back. He sat down before the mirror and applied some fresh lather to his left cheek.

"Holes in his pockets," Flynn said.

"Broke?"

"Not even a nickel for a once-over," he said, scraping his chin.

"What's the cost of a haircut?"

"A dime and up—up when they've got it."

"That's cheap enough," I said.

"Cheap is right for work by a graduate of the

Kansas City Barber College. A guy has to work cheap and fast for a living these days. O.K."

The House of David scored two runs on bunched hits off the Bismarck pitcher. The Negro sat up.

"Just look at those ball-playing fools!" he shouted. "They're right up in the big-time league!"

Flynn wiped his razor and felt his face.

"Whiskers, eh? O.K."

The locomotive whistle tooted like a fog-horn. Half a dozen men and boys got up from the embankment grass and stretched. A rumble ran through the string of cars as the engineer took up the slack in the couplings. A moment later the wheels began turning eastward.

The half a dozen men and boys swung up the sides of the cars. The Negro and the barber were watching the pitcher fan a Bismarck batter.

"Going East?" I asked Flynn as the train began gathering momentum.

"East and West, it's all the same. I can get mine anywhere between the Lakes and the Rockies."

"Save anything?"

"Save? Sure! I save more on the N.P. than I did working in the Palmolive Building in Chicago. Sure, I save. I've got it planted all the way from St. Paul to Spokane. O.K."

The train was passing at an increasingly rapid rate of speed. The faces of men and boys standing upright in coal gondolas, lying on flats, and sitting with their feet dangling over the sides of freight cars, were flashing past faster than they could be counted.

"No family to take care of?" I said.

"None for three years," Flynn the Barber said. "I had to drop my family when I took to the N.P. My wife and kids couldn't see the N.P."

Flynn, the Negro, and I watched the caboose rattle past.

"The wife and kids couldn't see the N.P.," Flynn said. "I don't know that I blame them any. O.K."

CHAPTER VI.

AFTER EIGHTY YEARS

THE gray-bearded old man shuffled out of the twenty-five-cent hotel and made his way to the curb. For five minutes he fumbled with the torn opening in his coat, trying to extract from it a small package wrapped in tough brown paper. The young men on the corner watched him disinterestedly.

Somebody with a pearl gray hat tilted on the back of his head hurried past. Half a dozen steps away he turned for a moment and called back.

"Hello, there, Cap!"

His attention distracted, the old man's fingers ran from the torn pocket to the top of his head. He scratched the mat of gray hair bound under the bedraggled cap.

The other man hurried on, turning out of sight down Front Street. The Fargo, North Dakota, business day was over.

Cap moved unsteadily across the pavement, bumping into the brick wall of the hotel. With a glance at the building he shuffled back to the curb as quickly as he could.

The package in the lining of his coat again drew his whole attention. The young men on the corner appeared to be interested only in what they were saying to each other.

All at once Cap jerked, tugged, and twisted the coat-lining and package; he began to swear at it in a husky roar. The young men picked up their ears.

"Hello, Cap!" one of them said.

"Taking up wrestling, Cap?" another one said.

For a moment the old man's fingers wavered between the package and the top of his head. Finally he dropped the twisted lining and raised both hands to his cap. He jerked it off. A cockroach fell on the pavement at his feet. For several seconds it lay on its back, kicking its feet into the air, and at last succeeded in turning over. It darted out of sight into the littered trash of the gutter.

Cap stood scratching his head with one hand while he shook the cap with the other. He was swearing hoarsely to himself.

The group of young men turned and watched his actions. Presently one of them strolled over and leaned against a lamp post.

"Why don't you get wise to yourself, Cap?" he asked.

The old man did not appear to have heard or even seen him. He swore for his own release alone, shuffling from one foot to the other, but not moving anywhere.

"All you have to do is go over to the Transient Relief, and they'll fix you up, Cap."

Cap began feeling in his pants pockets, on the back of his neck, and inside the lining of the headpiece. He paid no attention to what was being said.

"There's no sense in you old-timers bumming nickels and dimes any more, and flopping in these two-bit joints. Get wise to yourself, Cap, and take things easy. The Transient Relief will fix you up with a bunk and an eating card. Go on over there and get fixed up. You don't have to panhandle any more. The Government is handing out any kind of ticket you can ask for."

The old man replaced the cap on his head and began once more trying to extract the package. He mumbled unintelligibly to himself. The young man shrugged his shoulders and went back to the group on the corner.

"To hell with him," the fellow said. "You can't tell him nothing. If he wants to beg all day for a couple of dimes, that's his lookout. You'd think these old gray-bearded codgers would know a good thing when they saw it."

Cap, with a final twist, disengaged the package. It came out torn and wrinkled. He ripped off the paper and took out a bun and began munching on it. The brown paper fluttered away in the breeze.

After the roll was eaten, Cap wiped his hands and shuffled towards the corner. He was mumbling to himself.

At the corner he held out a hand, palm upward.

"Help an old man," he said, the words feeble and thin trickling through his whiskers.

"No hard feelings if you ain't got it," he said. "Just a nickel or dime or anything. Help an old man."

Nobody in the group said anything then. The fellow who had spoken to him several minutes before stared at Cap's ragged coat and pants. They all drew back a little.

The thin earth-colored hand, palm upward, followed them.

"Help an old man," he repeated.

Somebody took a wad of chewing gum out of his mouth and dropped it into Cap's hand. Cap's fingers closed over the sticky gum; then oaths trickled weakly through his discolored gray beard as he wiped his hand on coat and pants.

"Beat it, Cap," one of them said; "if you haven't got enough sense to stop panhandling on the streets and let the Government fix you up, you ought to crawl off somewhere and die."

The old man shuffled off down Front Street, holding forth his thin earth-colored hand, palm upward. He swayed forward into the direction of a figure approaching him.

"Help an old man," he said once more.

CHAPTER VII.

OUR GARDEN OF EDEN

I'M HARVESTING sixty bushels of corn to the acre this fall, and by the time I get ready to sell it looks like I'm going to make more money this year than I ever did before. I thought for a while I was going to have to wait for the Government to get the corn prices going upward, but the dry weather all around us stepped in and did more good than anything else could have done.

"Old Iowa never fails us. There can be too much dryness, or too much rain, everywhere else, but the Lord seems to favor Iowa and stops the plagues at the state line. They say the southern border counties of Iowa got nipped this year, but the drouth didn't do a mite of damage in the Garden of Eden. It's pretty near a disgrace to have a dozen or so counties down there living on Federal emergency relief, but I guess that's all the more reason why us up here in the Garden of Eden ought to feel proud of ourselves.

"Upper Iowa is God's favored country, if there ever was any. He looks after us like the Government could never hope to do. It's a pity everybody can't live here, but there wouldn't be room for them and us, too; and as it is, it's pretty hard to keep people out so we can have it to ourselves.

"I wrote a letter to my boy over in France just two nights ago, telling him not to worry about having enough money to keep him in good style. He's been living over there in Paris for two years now, and he's getting along fine. He's taking up writing for a career. Of course there is plenty of money on the farm, but he decided he could make nearly as much being a writer. He figures he'll be making ten thousand a year, after he spends another year there catching on to how it's done. Just before he decided to go over there, his classmate at Harvard tried to persuade him to stay in the United States, and maybe take a newspaper job to begin with; but my boy knew what he was doing when he decided to go over to France where everybody goes to learn writing.

"I've got a girl traveling in that part of the world, too; she's not learning anything like that, because she wanted to get married and nothing else. She figured out the thing she wanted to do was to travel all over Europe and meet the kind of people she wanted to marry into. The last letter I had from her said she was interested in a foreign fellow she met in Italy. I couldn't figure out from the letter if it was anything serious or not, but you never can tell what will come of it.

"I'm thankful to the Lord for setting me down here in the Garden of Eden. Just the other day I rode to Mason City and talked it over with some of the leaders of our church, and told them I wanted to show my appreciation the best I could. After we talked a while, I wrote out a check for a thousand dollars and handed it to our leaders to be put into our foreign mission fund. We've got a lot of missionaries over in

China, winning the heathens to our side, and I was proud to give what I could. I sort of felt sorry for them all my life, and every time I start thinking about the heathen Chinese over there in China I feel it my duty to give what I can in the way of money.

"For the past nine years I've been spending six months of the year out in Long Beach, California, which is, next to Iowa, the finest spot on earth. I've made a lot of friends out there, among people just like myself, and we have a club of our own right in Long Beach. I tell myself sometimes that I'm wavering about settling down out there for the rest of my life. I guess I am, at that. To my way of thinking, God only made two favored spots on the earth, and they are Iowa and Long Beach, California. Long Beach is just like Mason City had been picked up and carried out there and set down beside that beautiful blue ocean.

"I've been reading accounts of the drouth in all the states surrounding us, and I'm pretty well up on the subject. The whole trouble is that people made the mistake of settling down in the

Dakotas, Nebraska, and elsewhere, instead of settling down in Iowa. But then I get to thinking if they had all done that, there wouldn't be room enough here for us Iowans. So I guess it's just as well as it is.

"Lately I've got tired of reading so much in the papers about the dryness surrounding us, and when night comes I pick up one of the magazines instead. I've been a subscriber to the one called *The New Yorker* right along, and I get more pleasure out of reading it than anything else I know of, because it has stories all through it about just the kind of people I know in Mason City and Long Beach. I've got another favorite one now, too, called *Esquire*. It's got a lot more funny pictures and jokes in it than any other piece of reading matter you can find anywhere you look. I've subscribed five years ahead, so I won't miss getting it, even for one number. I nearly always buy an extra copy at the newsstand and give it to one of my friends, whether I happen to be in Mason City or Long Beach, California.

"The drouth you read so much about in the

papers these days is going to bring me a lot more money for my corn this fall than I expected to get, and I guess I ought to be real proud of being an Iowan living in the Garden of Eden. It's disgraceful the way the southern border counties got nipped, though. The only thing I can lay the blame of that to is that down there Iowa touches on Missouri. If it wasn't for that, the whole of Iowa would be as fruitful as my own acres."

CHAPTER VIII.

PICKING THE OMAHA DUMP

IF YOU live in downtown Omaha, Nebraska, there are several ways of reaching the city dump. You can take a street car or bus to South Omaha and walk a few short blocks to the grounds, you can walk the entire distance, or you can hitch-hike. The cheapest, quickest, and most satisfactory means by all odds is hitch-hiking; because the State Highway Department has constructed an up-to-date road to Lincoln that passes within a few yards of the dump.

Dump-picking in Omaha, as in all of America's cities, is an occupation as old as the city itself; but within the past three years, in Omaha for one, the field has become overcrowded. Moreover, the city of Omaha has failed to provide sufficient pickings for the increasing num-

ber of families that look to the dump for their
sustenance. The quality of the refuse has fallen
off rapidly since the latter days of the '20s, and
the quantity has dropped to less than one half
its 1930 tonnage. Those who look forward into
the coming winter see slim pickings ahead.

As early as the summer of 1934 the pickers
were deserting the contemporary dumpings of
the city and excavating in the area of the 1928-29
refuse. A comparison of the present era with
that of the near past reveals that in the cate-
gory of men's shoes, for example, the discarded
footwear of 1928-29 had badly worn outer soles,
whereas in 1934 the people were walking on their
uppers.

Ed Murdock is one of the discouraged pickers
of the 1934 dump. Since 1931, when he lost his
thirty-five-dollar-a-week packing plant job, he
has led a precarious existence. He has seen the
pickings go from bad to worse. Today he earns
a few cents gathering scraps of metal and selling
them at a junk yard. But his eyes grow dim and
his body stiff; he is losing much of the metal

which he considers is rightfully his to younger men who are quicker of eye and body. He is steadily falling behind in competition with the gangs of thirty-year-olds who can make a clean sweep of the dump in two or three hours and not leave half a pound of scrap iron behind them.

West of the' dump a two-story piano-box house is being roofed and sided with oblong lengths of tin. An old man by the name of Gates has taken squatter rights on a plot of fill and he is weatherproofing his house with beaten-out tin cans. Gates was getting old, and the walk from his house two miles away was more than he could stand; he decided to build and live within a stone's throw of his work. He has already constructed a heater from a five-gallon steel barrel, and the several lengths of stove-pipe arrived in the June dumpings. As soon as he is able to complete the ratproofing of the lower walls and floor, he will be prepared for a hard winter ahead.

You walk back to where Ed Murdock is at

work and stand around a while. Ed pries into the
dump, poking the end of his steel-tipped stick
into the refuse. There is a muffled tingle, and he
reaches down, burrowing with long, thin fingers,
into the mass until what looks like a former
objet d'art is revealed. Ed straightens up a little
and gazes at the five pounds of corroded metal
that represent the features of three tailless monkeys. Slowly he turns them over, fascinated by
the spell they cast over him, weighing them
nervously first in the right hand and then in
the left.

Ed glances up and looks you in the eyes ques-
tioningly. As you reach to examine the find, he
jerks it away and holds it close to his chest
while his pale blue eyes search you from head
to toe. After a few moments, satisfied that he
has never seen you on the dump before and convinced by firm assurances that you will not take
advantage of him, he allows you to examine it
in your own hands.

You rub the tarnish from the base of the object and find an inscription. It says SEE NO
EVIL—SPEAK NO EVIL—HEAR NO EVIL.

You read it to Ed. He asks you to read it a second time.

A thin smile breaks the lines at the corners of his mouth. He reaches for the object and begins rubbing it with his worn fingers. Slowly the grime of the dump is transferred to his hands.

"What do you think it is?" you ask.

Ed scrapes the top of one of the heads with his thumb-nail. A dull coppery sheen appears. Ed lowers his eyes to the gleam while his thumb-nail continues scratching at the monkey's head.

"It might be—maybe," he says after a while.

"Copper?"

Ed nods hopefully.

"I sure hope it is," you say.

"Me too," Ed says.

You take out a pocketknife and offer to scrape the surface for him. Ed takes the knife from you and scrapes it himself, careful not to shave off any of the precious metal.

"It's five pounds of something," you say reassuringly.

Ed looks up quickly from his task.

"I hope so," he says.

You are bewildered for a moment.

"You mean you hope it weighs five pounds, whether it's copper or not?"

Ed grins like a boy, nodding his head up and down.

CHAPTER IX.

DAYBREAK ON THE PLATTE

THE Jones farm on the Platte River in Central Nebraska occupies eighty-five acres of land, almost equally divided into tillage and pasturage. The wheat crop on the uplands has dwindled in yield for three years, but in the bottom lands the corn is higher than a man's head, and forty bushels, or more, will be gathered to the acre.

At dawn a light mist hung over the Platte and the bottom lands. But in the first warm rays of the sun the moisture vanished, and the air was once more like a searing blast from an open-hearth furnace.

The Jones' house was half a mile up from the river, identified by one lone tree that looked dwarfed in the treeless horizon. A little after sunrise the household began to stir. One of the boys stumbled sleepily out the kitchen door with a milk pail and went as far as the barn-yard fence. He leaned against the gatepost for a while, rubbing his eyes.

Smoke suddenly emerged from the kitchen chimney. Ten feet above the chimney top it evaporated in the air like steam on a hot day.

Jones came to the front door, shoes in hand. He rubbed his sleep-clouded eyes before saying anything. The sun smote him full in the face.

"Breakfast'll be along after a while," he said.

He sat down and laced his shoes.

"That's a nice crop of corn down by the river," the visitor said.

"Maybe so," Jones said. "But what's it going to amount to, anyway? There's no money in farming any more."

"A man ought to be satisfied to make a living these days, oughtn't he?"

"Oh, I guess he ought," Jones said. "If he don't, the Government'll make it up for him some way or other."

"Suppose there wasn't any Government to help people out—what would happen then?"

The tired farmer ran his fingers through his hair and rubbed his eyes.

"That's different," he said. After a moment he laughed a little, chuckling to himself. "No need to worry about that as long as we've got a Government to help out, though."

The sun had come up the Platte and was shining down upon Nebraska. The country, except for the green bottom lands on each side of the river, lay exposed to another day of summer sun. The grass-brown uplands and hills were beginning to shimmer in the heat already.

"With all that corn and forage down there, you won't have to ask the Government for anything," the visitor suggested.

"That?" Jones said, waving a hand towards the corn. "Why, I'm just sitting here now waiting for it to get ready to pull so I can haul it off. I'm looking forward to a good price for that corn this fall."

"All of it?"

"Just about," Jones said. "I'm counting on that corn."

"It looks to me as if you'd have enough corn and fodder to feed your stock all winter, and maybe have a little left over to sell in the spring."

Jones looked sharply at the visitor.

"I can get me a loan for the feed I'll need. The Government makes feed loans on milk cows, mares, and sows. I've been talking to the Government man about that. He told me just a few days ago that I wouldn't have no trouble getting feed loans on my stock this winter."

"I can't see how you'll be any better off in the end," the visitor said. "Wouldn't it be better to keep your corn and forage crop and use it yourself, instead of going into debt to the Government for feed?"

"The Government has got plenty of money to spare. It's the Government's duty to help out the farmers. The Government is handing out money all the time, and I ain't one to be bashful about asking for what others are getting, either."

Jones and the visitor sat in silence for a while,

each looking out across the dry country. In the distance were farms that were without river bottom lands; cows, horses, and pigs had been turned into the corn fields to eat the stunted stalks that had failed to produce so much as a nubbin of grain. When the corn fields were stripped clean, there was no other food within sight for the stock. If the cows, horses, and hogs ate anything after that, it would be hay and corn from Illinois and Indiana.

"You expect the price of corn to be up this fall?" the visitor asked finally.

"I figure on it," Jones said determinedly.

"But how about the prices of other things this fall. Won't higher prices for flour and shoes and such things cancel out the gain you get for your corn?"

The tired farmer got up and walked out into the yard. He thought for several moments before he replied.

"You might be right about that, but you oughtn't to be," he said. "Anyway, I figure I can make me a good-sized sum of money on my corn. Nobody's going to talk me out of getting what I can out of it."

The farmer and the visitor walked across the yard towards the barn. The rear end of an automobile that averaged ten miles to the gallon of gasoline jutted out from a shed.

"See that car, there?" Jones pointed. "Now, how in the world would I buy gas for it if I didn't sell my corn this fall? The Government hasn't figured on providing that yet, to my knowledge."

The visitor shook his head.

"That's right," he replied. "The Government hasn't said a word about making gasoline loans, yet."

CHAPTER X.

A TABLELAND FARMER

TEN miles west of Beatrice, Nebraska, on the broad land lying between the Little and Big Blue rivers, the sun had set. Along the roadside a man was mowing thistles and weeds and stray tufts of grass. Behind him a boy raked the forage into windrows.

"This is the first time in my life I ever thought a weed was good for anything," the farmer said. "And who ever would have thought a man would be hauling Russian thistles into his barn?"

"Will your horses and cows like it?" the other man asked.

"They've been eating all they could all summer long, whether they're crazy about it or not. Along about next New Year's Day it's going to come in mighty handy. You can't expect an animal to fatten on it, but nobody's asking that. If we keep alive, it's a help."

The boy crawled through the fence and went off across the barren wheat field to let down the bars at the pasture gate. Several horses and a colt were grazing in the pasture, finding here and there something to nibble. The cows, at sunset, were coming home.

The farmer stopped and whetted the scythe for several minutes. There was not much more to mow on that side of the road.

"There's a lot of discouraged farmers in the country these days," he said. "Somehow, I just can't get one of those long sad looks to come on my face. It looks like nearly everybody else I know had them pretty close under the skin all along, for otherwise I can't make out how they managed to get them all at once."

He stroked the cutting blade lightly several times and dropped the whetstone into his pocket.

"Maybe your neighbors were harder hit by the drouth than you were."

"I wouldn't say that. I didn't have a drop more rain than anybody else between here and

Beatrice. I had just as many, if not more head of stock to care for as anybody else I know. And it's likely that I've got fewer acres of pasture than any of the rest, excepting maybe one or two. No, everybody in this part of Gage County was treated alike as far as I can estimate."

"Are your neighbors—the other farmers—harvesting Russian thistles and weeds?"

"Some are, some are not. A lot of them said they wouldn't bother with the trashy stuff. They filled out applications for all kinds of Government loans, to buy feed mostly. They even cleaned out most of their stock, selling it to the Government when the Government offered to buy it. Right now, after all that, I can't see that they're any better off than I am. I still got all my animals, I've saved a little feed for the coming winter, and I don't owe a cent for any feed loans. Next spring I won't have to buy young stock at high prices, because I'm keeping what I've got —and taking care of them, too."

The farmer leaned his scythe against the fence and took out a pouch of smoking tobacco and a pipe. He filled it carefully, packing the flakes of tobacco into the bowl with a forefinger.

"You know," he said, "people as a whole appear to be getting a little soft, or something. It's not like it used to be at all. These days a man starts bellyaching as soon as he gets out of bed in the morning, keeps it up all through the day, and quiets down only after he falls to sleep at night. They carry on exactly like an old sore-head chicken. And right now, after they've reached this point, they complain about the Government for not giving them five days' work a week, when they're overpaid for the little work they do three days a week. I never was much of a forecaster, but, doggone it, you mark my words: it won't be so very long before they'll be complaining about the Government for not giving them one day off out of three, with full pay thrown in."

"There are a lot of people in the country who need all the help they can get," the other man said. "They would drop dead in their tracks of starvation, if the Government did not help them."

"Of course, there are," the tableland farmer said. "I'd be the first to stand up and make a demand for all the help they are in need of. But I'm talking now about people just like myself. I mean farmers who own forty to a hundred and sixty acres, and a dozen or so head of stock. There's no fattening on these farms for anybody now, man or animal, but there's work to do. You can pump water for the stock, or haul it from the river, instead of bellyaching about no rain falling. Some of them say they are too hungry to work. Maybe so; but I eat corn meal and hog sides every day, and it won't hurt the rest of them. Right now my ribs show through my hide, and my hunchbones stick out like cow horns, but I still manage to move around enough to forage what weeds and thistles there are."

He picked up the scythe and began swinging it close to the ground under the leaves and stems of weeds. The boy had let down the bars at the pasture gate, and the cows walked Indian file up the lane to the milking shed.

The farmer stopped and turned over a pile of thistle with the toe of his shoe.

"I may be wrong," he said, "but it looks to me like it took the drouth to bring out just how puny people are getting. I won't be calling names, but I know some farmers who were showing signs of letting their necks roll over the tops of their collars. And now, you—"

He made one more broad sweep through the weeds with his blade.

"Did you ever see or hear tell of a fat farmer who was worth his salt?" he asked.

Before the other man could reply, the farmer spoke again.

"Fellow, you know good and well you never did!"

CHAPTER XI.

SATURDAY NIGHT IN MARYSVILLE

An AUTOMOBILE that from all appearances came out of Detroit in the year 1918 rolled up to the gasoline tank in front of Bill's Garage in Marysville, Kansas. Eleven heads could be counted on the two seats.

Bill waved a hand but did not get up from the settee of burlap-covered springs on which he sat.

"The fellow is probably going to buy some gas," we said.

"We'll see," Bill said. "It's too soon to tell yet."

The woman in the car began quieting the children while the man climbed out to the street. Bill got up to meet him.

"How are you, Jim?" he said. He walked over

to the gasoline pump and leaned against it. "Howdy, Mrs."

The woman in the car turned around and slapped one of the children.

"Pretty well," she said.

"On your way home, Jim?" Bill asked.

"If I ever get there," he said. "I'm low on gas."

"Been in town today? I didn't see anything of you. Where'd you keep yourself all the time?"

"The old woman wanted a pair of leather shoes," Jim said. "I've been trying to locate a pair ever since early this morning. It looked like none of the stores wanted to sell a pair under a dollar ninety-eight. A while ago I got her fitted up in a pair of tennis shoes for forty-five cents, and I told her she'd have to make out with them this fall and winter."

"It sure is bad," Bill said. "And it don't look any better as time passes, either. It gets worse, if anything."

"I reckon it's getting worse," Jim said. "Least-aways, it's getting worse every day with me. I tell my family don't be taken back if we have to eat a couple of you this winter. It's a sure-God fact I ain't raised a bite to eat."

"How much gas do you think you'll need?" Bill asked.

The other man dug down into his overalls pocket and drew out a tight fist. When he opened it up, a nickle and several pennies gleamed in the light.

"Give me half a gallon this time," he said. "That ought to get me back home, but I don't know for sure." He handed Bill the money in his open fist. "Is that about right?"

Bill put the money in his pocket and pumped half a gallon of gasoline into the car's tank.

Jim cranked up and drove off. Some of the children leaned out and waved at us until they were out of sight.

"Not much profit in selling half a gallon of gas," we said.

"Not enough to notice," Bill said. "But what's a fellow to do—in a country where there hasn't been a noticeable rain for fourteen months?"

He had barely got the words out of his mouth before a bright yellow car dashed up to the pump and jerked to a stop over brake-locked wheels. A young fellow jumped out and lighted a cigar.

"Fill her up, Bill," he said. "I'm in a hurry tonight."

After the gasoline was in, Bill was handed a five-dollar note. Bill shook his head.

"I can't change that much," he said. "I'll have to go up the street for it."

The boy reached for the money, but Bill doubled his hand over it and backed out of his reach.

"I'll see you Monday," the boy said. "I haven't got time to wait for change now. Let me have it."

"No," Bill said, backing off, "I'll get it changed now."

The young fellow got into his car and followed him up the street.

Ten minutes later Bill came back to the garage. He sat down, crossed his legs, and spat all away across the pavement into the gutter.

"I never trust a man who's in a hurry, anyway," he said.

"That fellow must have a good job," we said. "He's got a well-kept car and five dollars."

"A lot more of us would have a five-dollar bill, if we had a forty-cents-an-hour job like he's got. There's nothing like working for the Government—if you can."

He spat across the pavement again, more forcefully than before.

"These young fellows with no family to support work three or four days a week for the Emergency Relief, at forty cents an hour, and a man like myself with a houseful of family to support can't raise enough money at one time to buy a twenty-four-pound sack of flour. There's going to be a heap of hungry people in this country this winter, and I wouldn't be surprised to see them going up to that Emergency Relief office and some day raising plain thunder about it.

"These young fellows can go up there now and put up a line of talk to those unmarried girls, and they get anything they ask for. You see them working on some little job for the Government three or four days a week and the rest of the time they ride around in their automobiles, shoot pool, drink beer, and throw money away in crap games just like it was plain paper.

"It don't do a bit of good to complain about it to the Government, yet. We got up a delegation not long ago, made up of people who are fed up with the way things are run, and went to Topeka to see the folks there about it. They told us if we didn't like the way things were run in Marysville, and didn't shut up about it, they'd take the very last one of us people off the relief rolls.

"That's the State of Kansas saying that, because they hand out the money the Government furnishes. Things now are just the same as ever, and the young fellows still ride around in their cars and throw away the relief money on pool games and beer drinking and crap shooting.

"But I'm telling you, Mister, you'd better watch out for trouble this winter, if it don't stop. I don't know what's likely to happen, but something's going to blow up—somewhere, somehow, sometime."

CHAPTER XII.

GRANDPA IN THE BATHTUB

SOME people said it had not rained a jugful in all Kansas in 1934, but Grandpa Price had caught ten gallons of rainwater that had fallen in Nemaha County since the first of the year. Of course, what little rain that did fall was not enough to mature the corn, keep the pastures green, and water the stock; but Grandpa Price had set tubs and pans under the eaves of the house and barn during three showers, and he had the water to show for it. He kept the water in bottles and jugs, corked tight against a single drop leaking out or evaporating.

In August Grandpa brought out his stored water and said he was going to take a bath.

It was not long before Grandpa Price was upstairs in the bathroom sitting as naked as a jaybird on the side of the tub.

Fanny, his daughter-in-law, had dinner all cooked and ready to serve, and the children were standing around the kitchen door begging to know when they could eat.

She went upstairs and knocked on the door. Grandpa Price yelled for her to come in if she wished to, and Fanny opened the door just enough to speak to him and to see what he was doing.

"It's dinner-time and the children are waiting for their meal," she said. "You'd better hurry and come downstairs."

Grandpa Price splashed his feet in the water, kicking it all over the room. The walls and floor were dripping wet.

"Look at the water, Fanny!" he shouted, splashing some of it in her face.

She closed the door and ran downstairs.

"Go tell your father to hurry to the house, Henry," she told the oldest boy.

Henry ran down to the barn where his father was still working. He had to pass Grandpa Price's crib of corn on the way, and he stooped and pushed his fingers through the wire matting and got a few kernels off a cob. He popped the corn into his mouth and began crunching it between his teeth. The five hundred bushels of yellow corn had been brought down from South Dakota by Grandpa Price when he moved in to live with his son Dale, and Fanny.

When Dale got to the house, he asked Fanny what the trouble was upstairs. She told him about Grandpa Price sitting on the side of the tub and splashing water all over the walls.

"Let's eat dinner before we try to get him out," Dale said. "Maybe by then he'll be ready to come out, anyway."

After dinner was over Grandpa Price was still upstairs, sitting with his feet in the water. He had been up there four hours.

The boys went down to the corncrib and worked a few more kernels through the wire netting. As long as Grandpa was up in the bathroom, they were not afraid of his getting after them for taking his corn.

The corn was six years old and, although his son and daughter-in-law had tried to persuade him to have some of it ground into meal, the key had not been turned in the padlock since the day it was brought in from South Dakota. Every

time the corn was mentioned, Grandpa said he
was keeping it for the lean years. He had lived
in the Dakotas twenty years, and he said he had
not lived there for nothing. The lean years were
still ahead, he told them.

When Fanny went upstairs at supper-time,
Grandpa Price's door was open and the room
empty of furniture. The bed and dresser were
gone, and even the chairs were missing. She ran
to the bathroom the first thing, and threw open
the door.

Grandpa Price was still in the bathroom. The
furniture had been stacked into the small room
until there was left only space for the tub.
Grandpa was sitting, naked, on the edge of it,
splashing water with his toes.

"I've never seen so much water since '96," he
said.

Fanny was about to shut the door and run
downstairs to tell Dale what Grandpa Price had
done when he reached out and grabbed her arm.
Still holding her, he reached somewhere behind
him and brought out a key. It was the long brass
key to the corncrib padlock.

"Here, Fanny," he said, thrusting it into her hand. "You take care of my corn for me while I'm up here, and dole it out carefully. Now that we've got all the water, the time's come to use it. I can trust you not to be wasting of it."

She took the key and backed out of the room before he could change his mind about the corn. The horses had not been grained for three months.

Downstairs Fanny ran to her husband and showed him Grandpa Price's key. There was no mistake about its being the key to the five hundred bushels of yellow Dakota corn.

He took the key and started to the crib. At the door he stopped, listening to the splashing of the water upstairs in the bathroom.

"It's a good thing we had those three little showers, after all," he said. "I don't know what would have happened to us if it hadn't rained at all this year."

He ran across the yard and opened the crib door and began throwing ears of yellow corn on the ground for the sow and loading his arms with it for the horses in the barn.

CHAPTER XIII.

LIKE 'SIXTY

BETWEEN forty and sixty per cent of the farmers in the primary drouth area are living on Government relief. In the face of a dark forecast, it is difficult to find many people who will hazard a guess that a decrease will come in the near future. If anything, it is generally expected that the coming months will bring a rise in the number of families on relief.

The drouth aggravated, in Kansas for one, a situation that already was serious. No state in the Union, certainly not Kansas, had escaped the nation-wide economic blight. In 1934 a new and devastating tragedy brought to new thousands the sharp pangs of hunger.

The Kansas farmer who harvested a bushel of corn to the acre in 1934 is the grandson of the

Kansas farmer who harvested a peck of wheat to the acre in 1860. The drouth of 1860, on a sparsely settled frontier, has repeated itself in a now densely populated state. Today in Kansas it is as dry as 'Sixty.

In 1860 the damage left in the wake of the disaster was wasted fields of corn and wheat. People, living few and far between, were somehow able to take care of themselves; and in a fit of unmatched generosity, the states of New York and Wisconsin appropriated several thousand dollars for the purchase of seed for Kansas pioneers. Today the Federal Government has undertaken to provide not only the seed, but the land and the sweat as well.

In the meantime the farmer, unhorsed and unfed, waits to see what the Government will do next. If the Government comes and supervises the planting and cultivating of his crops, he may well be prepared for the time when the Government will do the harvesting and marketing. By then the farmer will know that he has become the serf of a nation. He will have the choice of becoming a tenant farmer on Government land, binding himself to an insatiate land-lord, or of placing himself on perennial dole. Or the choice may not even be his to make.

The damage left in the path of the drouth is irreparable; crops and fields and stock have gone—they might be replaced. But the damage to men themselves, the loss of courage and self-reliance, can never be remedied.

The drouth area is like 'Sixty only in its pic-torial features. The stunted brown corn-stalks of today look the same as those of last century. The grassless pastures now are similar to the grassless pastures then. It is as hot as 'Sixty; dry as 'Sixty; and the barns are as empty as 'Sixty.

Socially there is no former era in America to which the present one may be compared. Today the children are as undernourished as—our only means of comparison—the children of the Sum-mer of 1934. Lack of sufficient food and medical attention is bringing a whole country to its knees; but the most devastating picture is that of thousands of children growing into maturity maimed for life by pellagra and malnutrition, by ignorance and defeat.

Society in its latter days abhors breadlines. Society, that is, which has sufficient bread of its own. The spectacle of seeing men, women, and children standing through the winter waiting for a hand-out of bread and soup is bad for trade, stagnates industrial dividends, and hampers individual freedom. The first impulse is to remove the breadlines from sight by means of contributing to a fund which will provide bread and soup.

The next step is the abandonment of breadlines, when their failure is apparent, and an attempt to let matters adjust themselves. Chaos inevitably follows, and dog eats dog. Then comes a cry for somebody to do something about it.

The Federal Government has taken up the game, making a third step. In place of community breadlines, bread and soup are brought into the individual home. The physical spectacle of breadlines is removed, but a breadline, whether composed of three hundred transients in Chicago, or seven members of the Brown family in Muscotah, Kansas, is a breadline still.

Kansans on primary and secondary Government relief rolls, whether working in a Government meat-canning plant or in a Federal mattress factory, are dissatisfied with their lot. They are canning beef to feed the hungry and stitching mattresses to bed the sick, but they know their employment is demanded by society's abhorrence of the breadline. They are victims of a selfish civilization. The undermining of their stamina makes them not grateful to, but angry with, a society which doles out relief in the form of poorly paid jobs.

CHAPTER XIV.

ALONG THE ROADSIDE

HALF a mile from Breckenridge, Missouri, two boys in a year-before-last roadster had turned off the traveled highway and parked in the shade of some trees. One of them had that day's comic section of the *Kansas City Star*, and every once in a while he picked it up and read it over again. The other boy, with his feet propped against the cowl, watched the cars go by.

"There's not much use of hanging around here looking for a job the rest of your life," the boy with the funny sheet said.

Both boys, under twenty, waved at a man they knew who was driving a truck towards Breckenridge. The driver waved back at them.

"Jim and I had a job last year, didn't we, Jim?" the boy with his feet on the cowl said.

"And look how long it lasted," Jim said, smoothing out the comic pages to look at them again. "Charlie thinks his Dad is going to find us a job soon, but he's been thinking that for two months already."

"I guess it's the same everywhere," Charlie said. "Have you seen any jobs go begging?"

I had to shake my head and say I had not.

Jim threw down the comic pages and watched the cars go by for a few minutes.

"What's the use of finding a job, anyway?" he asked. "As soon as you get one, you have to start worrying about losing it, because you're lucky these days to find one that lasts as much as a month. They fire you to hire somebody cheaper."

"We had a job out in Kansas working in the wheat harvest this year," Charlie said. "In about two weeks the fellow fired the whole bunch of us and hired another crew fifty cents a day cheaper. After we had taken a trip down into

Texas, we had just enough money left to get back to Breckenridge."

Jim picked up the comic sheet and smoothed it out.

"I'd rather travel around like that than stay at home and settle down to nothing. I've got a married brother who hasn't worked in two years. He's a carpenter, and used to make good money in St. Louis. Now he settled down and can't travel. All he does is sit around home waiting for something to turn up. I'm smart; I'm going to keep on the move. When I get through, I'll know a lot of the country, anyway."

"We're figuring on a trip to California next," Charlie said. "When we get a new set of tires and enough money ahead for the gas, we're going out for a couple of months. We've been nearly everywhere else in the country so far."

"I've been out of school three years," Jim said, "and I've worked about three months. What's the use of trying to get a steady job, expecting to hold it and settle down?"

Both boys watched the cars go by for a while.

It was late in the afternoon, and some of the automobiles passed with their lights turned on.

"Jobs are so scarce these days that about all that's left to do is working some kind of racket," Charlie said. "We could go out and pull some fast ones, too; but I don't like these hot jobs. I see too many of them get caught up with, and it goes pretty hard with them when they are caught."

"What kind of a racket can you work out here on the farm?" I asked.

Jim folded up the *Star's* comic section and slipped it under the seat. It was getting too dark to read without a light.

"You haven't heard about the cattle-buying racket?" Jim asked.

I shook my head and told him I had not been in Missouri very long.

"The Government is paying from ten to twenty dollars a head for cows—any kind of cows."

"They buy up the cattle from the farmers who can't feed them any longer," Charlie broke in. "They ship most of them up into Iowa to can the meat."

"Where does the racket come in?" I asked.

"You can take a truck and go out into the country on the back farms and buy up cows for five dollars a head, haul them into town, and the Government pays you anywhere from ten to twenty dollars apiece. They never pay less than ten, and if the cows look like anything at all, it's easy enough to get fifteen. All you have to do is turn over ten or fifteen head a day, and you stand to make fifty, seventy-five, or a hundred dollars on one day's work."

"It sounds easy," I said, "but don't the Government buyers ever catch on?"

Charlie laughed.

"That's when the racket gets hot," he said. "If they won't talk business, you have to shop around and find a buyer who is willing to be reasonable. After that, you would have to split the profit two ways."

"You have to work fast to make anything," Jim said. "The Government is on the watch all the time, and if they find anything funny going on, they make it pretty hot for everybody in on it."

"But the fifty or a hundred dollars a day is a lot of money, and a lot of people take a chance," Charlie said.

"Have you boys been in on it?" I asked.

"Us?" Charlie said. "Not on your life! We figure on traveling around and seeing the country. You wouldn't catch us handling a hot job. I'm too smart for that game. I'm going to see what the world looks like outside of Missouri."

CHAPTER XV.

ONE MORE DAY IN CHILLICOTHE

I CAME into Chillicothe, Missouri, at seven o'clock in the morning and stretched out on the cool green grass of the court-house lawn. There were not many people in the Square, but a man was sweeping off the steps of the Livingston County court-house, and another man crossed the street and stretched out on the grass a dozen feet away.

A grocery clerk opened up the store across the way and began carrying to the sidewalk some of the contents of the market. A Negro drove a wagon loaded with empty packing cases out of an alley, and two children arrived in the Square in a pony-cart to buy a loaf of bread.

It was still seven o'clock in Chillicothe. Two

95

men came from somewhere and sat down together on a bench on the court-house lawn. The
grocery clerk took one bite of an apple and
threw it into a trash box.

Some automobiles rushed through the Square,
going from one end of town to the other. A boy
rode down the street on his bicycle, blowing a
whistle. The man lying on the grass a dozen feet
away turned his head a little and watched the
grocery clerk hang up a stalk of bananas in the
doorway of the store.

I had come into Chillicothe at seven o'clock,
and it was still seven. A girl in a thin summer
dress hurried past on her way to the drug store
where she had a job. She turned and looked at
us lying on the grass at her feet. The fellow beside me watched her out of sight.

"What's the chance of picking up a job in
town?" I asked him.

The fellow only smiled.

Two lawyers hurried into the Livingston
County court-house. They had their pockets
and hands full of papers. They were working
on an important case. A few minutes behind

them came their secretary, hurrying along on
Louis XIV heels.

"Jobs scarce?" I said.

"Partner," the fellow said, shaking his head,
"me and you both."

"How long have you been looking for one?"

"Partner, I can't remember that far back."

"What's the trouble?" I asked. "Why aren't
there any jobs?"

The fellow smiled, looked across the street at
the stalk of bananas, and raised his chin off the
ground so he could speak.

"Overproduction, they say."

He smiled again, dropping his chin down into
the grass.

Over on the corner a boy began sweeping off
the sidewalk in front of the moving-picture the-
atre. Peanut shells, cigarette butts, and chew-
ing-gum wrappers flew into the air. Behind the
boy a red and yellow poster reached from the
pavement to the second-story window of the
building. A girl in a negligée pouted nine-inch
blood-red lips at a man wearing a street-corner

mustache. An eight-year-old boy stopped and studied the poster.

The fellow lying beside me on the grass reached behind his back and scratched himself. I thought it would be around eight o'clock, but it was barely a quarter after seven.

"I only need a job long enough to earn my way out of town," I said.

"Me and you both, partner," he said, smiling with a brief breaking of the lines around his mouth.

"There used to be jobs everywhere. A man could pick up a day's work with no trouble at all. He didn't have to worry about making a living."

"That's what used to be. There's two or three hundred waiting around town now, just like me and you, for a job to turn up. Sometimes one does. One."

"What's the trouble with everything, anyway?" I asked.

"Overproduction, they say."

Both of us laughed at the same time. There's something to laugh about, when you think it over a while and repeat it out loud two or three times. You laugh involuntarily, the same way that you can't help from sneezing once in a while.

Up the street came a farmer from the country, driving with care. He rode on three wheels of rubber and a steel rim. He had got up early that morning so he could spend the day wrangling a little credit from the merchants. He did not know which way to turn. 41342

The fellow beside me took out a sack of tobacco and some cigarette papers. He rolled one and handed me the makings.

I crawled a few feet on my stomach to reach the match he struck.

"What's your line of work?" I asked him.

"That's a hot one," he said. "I wouldn't have no more use now for a trade than I would for a flying-jenny. Back in other days I used to be a pretty good garage mechanic."

Across the street the grocery clerk ate a banana and threw the peeling into the street. In the window of the store next door a clock showed that in a few minutes it would be seven-twenty.

The fellow stretched on the grass beside me watched a sparrow hop across the lawn.

"Overproduction, they say," he muttered aloud.

The sparrow, frightened, fluttered out of sight into a tree top.

CHAPTER XVI.

THE THREE FACES OF MEN

NORTH of the Burlington Route tracks in Brookfield I came upon a man with a gold chain strung across his vest. He appeared to be a person of such importance that I hesitated to speak to him. He was standing in the shadow of the bank a moment before going inside to transact some business.

I hurried up to him before he could enter the building and asked him if he could tell me in a word what was the economic condition of Missouri.

"We are getting along better than anybody else. You ought to go to Kansas for information along that line."

I told him that in Kansas I was advised to come to Missouri. In Nebraska, I was told to go to South Dakota. From there, I was urged to go to North Dakota. In North Dakota, I was told Montana. In Montana, I was told to go to North Dakota, and the cycle began all over again.

"Everybody seems to think he is better off than the other person," I said. "Are you making a lot of money these days?"

He waved the bank book he held in his hand.

"How's business in Brookfield?" I then asked. "Dry weather hurt much?"

"Brookfield is an industrial town," he said. "What happens around us doesn't affect us much. I suppose it is a little dry in the country, but Brookfield gets along the same as ever. It's these towns that aren't blessed with industrial life that get hard hit by such times as these."

"Everybody working, I suppose."

"Not everybody, but nearly everybody. We get along pretty well in Brookfield, because it's an industrial town."

Somebody came up the street and ran into the man to whom I was talking. I backed away and left them.

Down the main street, across the Burlington

tracks, on the south side, a large crowd of men were standing in front of a former bank building. Inside there were even more men. Nearly all of them were between the ages of forty and sixty. Mingled with them were several women, nearer sixty than forty.

In one corner of the room a clerk at a table was interviewing a line of men that stretched to the door.

A man at the cashier's window was sorting some papers.

"What's this?" I asked him.

"The Missouri Relief and Reconstruction Commission office," he said.

"Many farmers on relief?"

"Fifty to sixty per cent of them are."

"Why?"

"In normal times they raise fifty to sixty bushels of corn to the acre. This year's crop is zero in seventy-five per cent of cases."

"What's the prospect for the winter?"

"A hundred per cent worse than right now."

"How is business in Brookfield?"

"You can see for yourself—inside this office and out on the street."

Out on the street the crowd was so thick around the relief office that there was barely enough room to pass through. A man in freshly washed and ironed overalls was passing around a petition of some kind. Everyone to whom he handed it signed with emphasis. Nobody asked what the petition was for, nor took the trouble to read it. It was a petition for something, and if enough people signed it, they might get something they were in need of.

A farmer drove up the street in a truck loaded with three milch cows.

"Where's the folks who buy cows for the Government?" he called to the crowd.

Somebody went out and told him what he wished to know.

A mile from the relief office a family was piling sticks of furniture into a broken-down truck. A boy was tinkering with the motor, trying to start it. The man carried the heaviest pieces of furniture to the truck and hurled them into it. A plywood dresser came to pieces and fell on the ground at his feet. He kicked the pieces out of his way.

The overalls the man wore were tied together with strips of cloth, and they flapped around his body like bunting. The rents in his clothes were so large that if he had appeared on the main street in Brookfield, north of the Burlington tracks, he probably would have been arrested for indecent exposure.

The woman carried a bundle of rags out of the shack and dropped them on the ground beside the truck. She went back inside for something more. A ten-months-old baby fed at her breast.

"Moving?" I asked the man.

All of them, including the grease-smeared boy and the bare-breasted woman, turned and stared. A girl came to the door and joined them. She held her torn dress together with her hands.

The man nodded to my question.

"Where to?" I asked.

"God knows," he said. "I don't."

When he finished, all of them went back to work.

CHAPTER XVII.

A COUNTRY THAT MOVES

Twenty miles from Springfield, Illinois, Frank Hanley fries hamburgers in his roadside lunch stand and listens to what is going on in the country. He said he learns more about what is happening, from what travelers tell him, than he does by listening to the radio.

He told about a man stopping in for a bite to eat a few days before and telling him that the Century of Progress Exposition in Chicago was going to run another year. The year before a man had told him the same thing, that the fair was going to run through 1934 as well as 1933, and he had not believed it. He said you can see for yourself what happened.

The man at the counter asked for some mustard and ordered another hamburger. Frank put it on the fire.

"Since the country started to move," Frank said, "everything has changed. Nobody settles down long enough to hold a steady job any more. Everybody gets on wheels and travels."

The man, between bites, asked how that was.

"It's just like the Eighteenth Century," Frank said.

"Is that something I ought to know about?" the customer asked.

"Don't you remember reading in history about how people then used to be on the road all the time? The inns were always full, all over Europe and England, and people traveled day and night."

"Uh-huh," the customer said, biting.

"And another thing I just learned," Frank said, "is that the Detroit Tigers are going to have a chance at the World's Series this year."

The man at the counter laid down his cup and saucer and pointed at the coffee urn. Frank filled it up.

"That's anybody's guess," the man said.

"Maybe so," Frank said. "But the fellow who told me that was the catcher."

"What catcher?"

"The Tiger catcher," Frank said.

Frank then told him about a family that had driven up to the door for something to eat just the day before, and who had been on the road a year and a half, and were still traveling.

"If you had any idea of the traveling people do in these days, you'd know how I find out so much," Frank said. "Travelers crisscross this country like rat tracks. It's exactly like the Eighteenth Century."

"That's a funny thing about that Eighteenth Century," the other man said. "I'd never heard about the Eighteenth Century before."

"That's what comes of getting your education over the radio," Frank said. "That's why I'm an educated man. I sit here and listen to travelers tell about the country, and then when I close up at night I read history."

The fellow at the counter wiped his face and called for a pack of cigarettes.

"That's a lot of foolishness," he said. "You

can't believe everything you hear. If you do, you get taken in more times than not."

"People zipping up to Chicago, down to New Orleans, across to Los Angeles, over to New York, everywhere in the country, day and night, rain and shine, keeps the country on the move and the tales fresh and reliable. If one man tells me a tale about something that happened in Texas, I can check up on him with the next half a dozen Texas travelers that stop for something to eat. In the Eighteenth Century tales got pretty wild because there was no way of checking up on them."

Frank leaned across the counter, watching the traffic on the highway out of the corner of his eye.

"A man from Alabama was in here yesterday and told me about a petition some men in a Government transient camp down there got up and sent to Washington. Those boogers in the camp sat around most of the day, with a lot of time on their hands to kill, and so they petitioned the Government to furnish them with a revival preacher. The Government had been sending around tickets to moving pictures every once in a while, but these boogers said they'd rather have a revival preacher than movie tickets."

The man on the stool looked for a moment as if he did not know whether to believe Frank or not.

"Well, since you probably heard about it before the Government had time to get the petition," the man said, "I don't guess you know if they got the preacher, do you?"

"Whether the Government got the petition or not, these boogers in the transient camp got the preacher, because two days after they sent it off, a preacher came in and settled down to live in the camp. Now they have preaching every night and all day Sunday."

The fellow on the stool shoved some money across the counter and got to his feet.

"That's better than the Eighteenth Century, isn't it?"

"I don't know about that," Frank said; "but I do know it's just like the Eighteenth Century."

"That's what's wrong with the country now," the other man said. "You people flood the country with tales like that, and people have got so they won't believe even their own grandmother any more."

"There's nothing wrong with the country," Frank said. "The country is all right. It's just like the Eighteenth Century."

The man went to the door and stopped. He turned around after a moment, flushed and angry.

"Say," he shouted, "what is this Eighteenth Century, anyway? What kind of a tie-up does it have with the Century of Progress?"

CHAPTER XVIII.

ON EXHIBITION

A BANANA pie-eating contest was to take place at three o'clock in Frank Buck's Jungle Camp at the Century of Progress in Chicago.

After several minutes' delay Frank Buck and his men brought out the three hundred individual pies and placed them on Monkey Island. The monkeys, one by one, began to sample the pies while the twelve hundred men, women, and children looked on. Between bites the monkeys looked at the people.

The elderly woman and her daughter were afraid they had missed the banana pie-eating spectacle, but the ticket seller assured them that they were in plenty of time.

Inside the Camp they had a difficult time

pushing through the crowd to get close enough to see what was going on. They could see the top of Monkey Island, which jutted like a dome a hundred feet into the air; but the lower level, close to the surrounding basin of water where the pies and monkeys were, was out of their sight.

Several newspaper photographers who had been taking pictures of the contest packed up and left, and the old lady and her daughter were just in time to squeeze forward and get their places at the railing.

"Well," the old lady said, "we did get here, after all. I still don't see how we ever got through all those crowds, though."

The daughter was so deeply engrossed—having only two eyes to see with—in following the movements of the three hundred monkeys that she paid no attention to what her mother had said.

"What are they doing, Frances?" the old lady asked, shaking her.

"Don't you see, Mama?" she said. "They are

eating the banana pies. Have you ever seen so many monkeys in your life?"

The woman's eyes finally adjusted themselves to the distance, and she was able to see something of what was taking place.

"Well, I hope we didn't come all the way from Denver just to look at three hundred monkeys," she said.

Several persons began tossing ripe bananas on the island, and the monkeys were much more pleased with them than they were with the pies. They began fighting over the bananas, pushing each other into the water, biting, and scolding.

"I've never seen such carrying-on," the old lady said.

The man in the crowd with the bag of bananas tossed the remaining ones on the island, and there was a mad scramble for the fruit. The lucky monkeys climbed to the top of the concrete island and ate the bananas unmolested. The unlucky ones sat and regarded the pies. One turned a pie over, inspected the crust like a bride, and tossed it into the water.

When all the bananas were gone, the monkeys

congregated on the sunny side of the island and toyed with the pies. Presently one picked up a pie and hurled it at the crowd. All the monkeys looked up at the people who had laughed so loudly at the antic. When the laughter died down, another monkey picked up a pie and hurled it over the water at the crowd.

The old lady from Denver tugged at her daughter's sleeve, saying nothing. Her lips were firmly compressed, and her head was held a little more erectly than it had been previously. She tried not to look at the monkeys, but no matter how hard she tried, her eyes were continually drawn back to them.

She pulled once more at her daughter.

"Please, Mama, let's not leave yet," the girl said.

"Frances," the woman said, "this is no place for us."

The girl recognized a familiar expression on her mother's face. She could not disregard it, especially since they were in public. She begged to know what the trouble was.

The woman pointed at Monkey Island. The

gaze of the three hundred monkeys upon the people was unrelenting.

"Frances," she said, "those monkeys are looking at us."

The girl did not understand for a moment.

"I came here to look at them," the old lady said, "not to be looked at. I never dreamed they would look at me like that. I feel just like a monkey myself. I can't stay in this place another minute."

The daughter attempted to persuade her mother to stay just a few minutes longer, but the old lady turned and began trying to push her way towards the exit. The girl followed her.

"But, Mama," she pleaded, "we came here to see them. Why can't we stay?"

"Don't talk to me about staying in such a place. That man who put those monkeys there did it just so they could look at us. It's an outrage."

They got halfway through the crowd, and the girl tried once more to persuade her mother to stay a little longer.

"No," the old lady said. "Positively not! I

never dreamed I'd come all the way from Denver to show myself to three hundred monkeys. Why, I feel positively indecent!"

Giving up, the girl looked back for one more view of Monkey Island. The woman, seeing her, grasped her by the hand and pulled her through the gate.

CHAPTER XIX.

JOE JENDRO

FROM Whiting to East Chicago, from Hammond to Gary, the Indiana dunes support the weight of the mid-continent's oil and steel. For fifty years the ore and crude oil for half of America have been processed on the dunes, becoming stoves and plows and gasoline and kerosene for fifty million people. The ore and oil arrived, and the stoves and gasoline were dispatched; but in Whiting, East Chicago, Hammond, and Gary were left heaps of slag and swamps of sludge to cover the dunes. The sand does not drift any more.

Looking down from an airplane a mile high, the oil refineries and steel mills look like a blackened, fire-gutted forest. Thin wisps of smoke rise from the factory smokestacks, look-

ing as if the trees were still smoking from their
ruin.

On the ground men and boys have gathered
around the gates of the plants. At an oil refinery
there are between two and three hundred persons; clustered in front of a guarded barbed-
wire gate of a steel mill are another two
hundred. Uniformed guards, armed with blue-
steel weapons, carry the keys that will not turn
for every man. All day and all night the crowd
of job-seeking men before the gates swells and
contracts. After a morning of waiting to find out
if he is going to be hired for a few hours of
labor, a man leaves; two other men arrive in
his place and take up the vigil. In front of a factory gate that swings open, calling forty men to
work, a hundred are left to wait another day,
another week. The gate clicks shut; the guards
hurl back the jeers, the threats, the obscenities
of job-hungry men.

Joe Jendro spat upon the refinery gate, dug
his hands into his pockets, and turned towards
home. There were other men going in the same
direction, other men passing him who went the

other way, but he had nothing to say to anybody. He was hungry, he was out of smoking tobacco, and his wife was coming down with another baby.

At the store, a block from his home, he went inside and laid the thirteen cents on the counter. It was all he had, and it might be a week before he would have that much again. The clerk asked him what he wished for the money.

"A loaf of bread, and a sack of tobacco, and damn you," Jendro told him.

The clerk glared at him, looking for a moment as if he would accept the challenge. Meeting no response in Jendro's vacant gaze, the clerk picked up the money and threw the bread and tobacco at him.

"You can stay out of here after this if you can't keep your mouth to yourself," the clerk said.

Jendro the puddler, the oiler, the punch-pressman, the spittoon cleaner, and everything else he had ever been, leaped at the clerk's throat. A blow on the head with an iron box-opener stood Jendro off. He turned and walked out the door.

When he got home, his wife was lying down. She had covered her face with a handkerchief to save herself the exertion of brushing off the flies. The one room in which they lived had not been cleaned that day.

Jendro threw the loaf of bread on the table and walked over to the bed where his wife lay. He picked up the handkerchief and woke her from sleep.

She did not ask him if he had worked that day. She had not asked him that for six months, maybe a year. She had forgotten how long.

"Where's he?" Jendro said.

His wife turned and looked around the room. She shook her head.

The chair by the window where Jendro's father sat when he was not lying on the floor was empty. The old man was not in the room; it was the first time since last winter that he had left it.

Jendro got the butcher knife and cut off a

third of the loaf of bread. He sat down in his father's chair and began eating it.

Presently it got dark, and Jendro's wife told him he ought to go look for his father. Jendro sat by the window looking down into the street for another half hour. He filled his pipe again, but he had used his last match. He got up and left.

At the store on the corner he walked in.

"Give me a match," he said.

The other clerk had left and another man was in his place.

"Get out of here, Jendro!" he shouted. "Get out before I throw you out!"

The clerk rushed around the corner of the counter and shoved Jendro almost off his feet. He went flying through the door to the sidewalk.

Ziebarth, who lived in the room over Jendro, came down the street. He had just got up from a nap.

"Your father is up there in the room where that Cysewski used to live," he said.

"I've been looking for him," Jendro said. "What's he doing up there?"

"Your father came up there and told me he was going to lay down and take a good rest," Ziebarth said. "I asked him why he came up there and laid down in an empty room, and he said he wanted to be where he'd have time enough to finish dying before you came along and moved him."

Jendro asked for a match and lit his tobacco. Ziebarth went down the street towards the factory where he applied every night for a job. When the tobacco was thoroughly afire, Jendro turned and spat against the window of the store. Digging his hands into his pockets, he started out to move his father.

CHAPTER XX.

A LIVING TO MAKE

PAT GLENN is twenty years old, and he had saved enough money in eight years to build and pay for a gasoline filling station of his own. It is in the country near Fremont, Ohio, on the Toledo highway. The station is no fancy catch-penny; it was built neither in the inflated form of a rooster, nor like a derby hat.

When he graduated from high school, Pat had a few hundred dollars saved. With it he could have gone to college for at least one year, possibly two. But he decided that he was not suited to receive a college education. It took him a year to decide what to do, and then he set out to accomplish it. He built a filling station, paid for the ground and plant, and opened for business.

124

That was a year ago, and he is in business still.

Next year he is going to vote for the first time, when he will become of age, and already he has drawn up the issues of the elections. When the candidates for office announce themselves, he will present his views to them, rather than listen to their platforms.

He has his feet pretty well on the ground for a boy twenty years old, raised an orphan.

The drawings of the winners in the Irish, Canadian, and British sweepstakes do not interest him, because he does not invest his weekly earnings in an attempt to make a hundred thousand dollars overnight. He would like to marry and build a house of his own to live in. He is not interested in 1000-to-1 horseracing odds, nor in 10-to-1; he believes he is an ordinary, average human being, and he wishes to work and live like one.

Several months ago a man drove up to his filling station and bought a tankful of gasoline. They talked for a few minutes, and the man offered to make Pat a partner in a business deal. Pat asked him what the proposition was.

When the man had finished explaining, Pat shook his head. He was not interested in gasoline bootlegging any more than he was in the drawings of the Army & Navy Sweepstakes. The man took out a pencil and some paper and began putting down figures to show how much money Pat could make in a few months. He said that with Pat's volume of trade he could make more in a month, selling bootlegged gasoline, than he could in a year selling legal, tax-paid gas and oil. He even offered to put up a hundred dollars of his own money to bet that Pat would make more profit the first week than he would in a month otherwise. Pat was not interested in the proposition.

Several weeks after that two men drove up in a Michigan car and took him to one side. They had a proposition to lay before him. Pat said he was not interested, but they insisted. Finally he told them to go ahead and explain it.

They wished him to sell them fifty gallons of gasoline that night at two o'clock, and to keep his mouth shut about it. Besides paying him for the gasoline, they would give him ten dollars to forget about it afterward. Pat told them he did not like the looks of things. They offered fifteen dollars, then twenty, and finally twenty-five. He said he was not interested.

The next day Pat read in a newspaper that an overland motor express had been highjacked of five new automobiles en route from Detroit to Wheeling, West Virginia. The robbery had taken place half a mile from his filling station at two o'clock in the morning. The two men who held up the driver were described so well that he recognized their description.

"I'm not getting rich," he said. "I'm just trying to make a living. Some weeks I do, and some weeks I fall behind. I'd like to get married in another year, if I'm able."

The house lot has been bought and paid for, but the money for the building material is yet to be earned.

"I thought I could sell a few other things to people who stop to buy gas and oil," he said. "Then I found out that what people would buy couldn't be sold at a profit. The State of Ohio demands fifty dollars a year for a license to sell cigarettes. I might be able to make fifty cents a week profit selling them, but I'd never make fifty dollars a year.

"There are a lot of us who could make a living, one way or another, if we didn't have to support a lot of people who make a profession out of politics. Taxes are just another racket now. It would be different if the State of Ohio were trying to keep cigarettes from being sold, especially to children; but they are sold to ten-year-old kids everywhere in the State.

"If Ohio wants to put a stop to the selling of bootlegged gasoline, the people who hold office will have to come down to earth and help those who are trying to make an honest living. If a man were hard up, don't you think he would sell bootlegged gasoline, instead of paying fifty dollars for a permit to sell half a dozen packs of cigarettes a day? The State of Ohio had better begin thinking about that while there is still time. It might be too late soon."

CHAPTER XXI.

BLACK DIAMONDS

THE use of anthracite coal continues to diminish. Oil-burning furnaces replace coal for heating purposes, hydro-electric energy replaces coal-burning generating plants, and bituminous coal is used to lower costs of factory operation. The Scranton, Pennsylvania, anthracite coal region still exists, and so do the miners —some way or other.

Everything would be all right—if the surplus miners could find something else to do, if they had unemployment insurance to live on, if they removed to South America, or if they committed suicide.

Instead, they sit in the doorways and windows of their tenements and look at us walking along the street. Some of us are working fairly regularly, down in the earth under the city of Scranton; we hurry past, trying not to meet their eyes, because we are afraid of the gloomy specter of abandoned hope we see there. Today we are lucky, because we are working; tomorrow our luck might change, and place us in the doorway of the tenement.

While there is still hope, we look forward to another day when a job will call us to work. When hope has gone, the future becomes merely a continuation of the present.

Coal will be mined under Scranton for many generations to come, but it will not make any difference, one way or the other, to John Stoa and his family. The seven of them have been blown to the four winds. It happened that in America John Stoa was one of the too many miners.

"Where is your wife, John?"

He shook his head indifferently. He had not seen her in two years, but she was in Scranton if she was still alive.

"She got hungry one day and left," John said.

"What can I do? I can't make food. I can't hold up my two hands and make it grow there."

There were two sons and three daughters, all now over eighteen.

"Where is the oldest boy, John?"

He did not know, but he thought he was in a prison somewhere. Possibly the Eastern Pennsylvania Prison at Philadelphia. Or it might be Sing Sing, in New York. He was not sure. The boy had lost his job with a trucking company. He bought a pistol and got on the train and went somewhere. John thought it was either Philadelphia or New York. He was not sure. But he did not think they had electrocuted the boy.

"They put him in jail. Ten years. Twenty years. I don't know. Maybe ninety years. I don't know."

The bare tenement was cold. As long as the sun shone against the window he could keep warm. Before long, when the sun stopped shining and when the snow came, he would go out with a sack and pick up some coal from the abandoned dumps.

"Is the other boy here?"

"I see him sometimes," John said. "I don't know what he does. I never asked him. He worked underground for a while, but I don't know if he is working now."

"What's your oldest girl's name, John?"

"Anna."

"Where is she?"

"Anna got married to a miner, but he couldn't work, either. Something got wrong with his lungs. He couldn't spit water like me and you. He spit blood all the time. He couldn't work any more."

"Where is Anna now?"

"Anna had two babies at one time and died. They buried her somewhere. I don't know where it is."

"What happened to the babies, John?"

He shook his head, jerking his shoulders a little.

"What are you going to do, John?"

"Nothing," he said quickly. "I finished long time ago. Wound-up, finished, done. Nothing no more for John Stoa."

"Don't you wish to get a job?"

"What good does that do? I don't get one."

"Going to sit here and look out the window all the time?"

"Sure," John said. "No job, nothing to do. Can sit here and look out."

"Who pays your rent? The city, the state, or the Government? Who pays it for you?"

John did not know. Nobody ever told him. For a while some people came to see him, asking him a lot of questions about his former jobs in the mines under Wilkes-Barre, Pittston, and Scranton. That was a long time ago, and he did not remember anything else.

"Where are the other two girls, John?"

One of them washed dishes in a hotel for a while, and then she went off with a man and he never saw her after that.

The other one was killed in Buffalo. He did not know how it happened.

"Have you any other kin, John?"

"Nobody," he said. "Nobody but John Stoa now."

"If the mines opened up again, and there were jobs for everybody, would you go back to work?"

"I finished," John said. "I sit in the window and look out. I wound-up, finished, done."

CHAPTER XXII.

WHEN LABOR SPEAKS

IN A Lawrence, Massachusetts, lunchroom they were discussing the impending textile strike, scheduled to begin the following day.

"I make twenty-eight dollars a week, and I'm satisfied with that for five days' work," the Englishman said. "But I can't be satisfied with myself if I don't do all I can to help people who don't make enough to live on."

"Are you going to walk out tomorrow?" the lunchroom owner asked. "It's bad for business."

"You can bet your last bottom dollar I am," the Englishman said. "If I was making half of what I am, I'd want other workers to walk out for me, wouldn't I?"

"It's bad for business," the owner said. "I've gone broke two times in strikes in the past twelve

134

years. One more time and I'll stay broke. It's too hard to get started again these days."

The Irishman banged on the table with his fist.

"If I was making seventy-five dollars a week, which I once did, I'd walk out tomorrow just the same," he said. "There never has been a strike yet that didn't do a world of good. It keeps the mills from walking over you. If it wasn't for strikes, right now all of us would have chains clamped around our ankles, and the other end would be welded to the mill. That's what not striking would bring."

The Yankee put his foot down.

"Anybody in these days and times who won't accept a chance to work is a fool," he said. "He ought to be locked up for committing a crime. It's a crime to walk out of a mill when the own-ers are willing to hire. And there'll be enough loyal workers to keep the mills going, too. Most people have got foresight enough to work when they can."

The owner of the lunchroom nodded enthusi-astically.

"See there?" he said. "What did I tell you? Now, can't you see what people with sense will do?"

The Englishman would have none of it.

"If the workers had never taken their right to strike, there is not a man in this restaurant who would have a dollar of his own. We'd be working for fifty cents a day, or maybe less than that. And right now there are workers getting only fifty cents a day, and maybe less. If the rest of us don't step in and help them win the strike, it won't be so very long before we'll be getting fifty cents a day ourselves."

"Every man ought to work when a job is offered him," the owner said. "And I believe there are enough loyal workers in Lawrence and everywhere else where there's a cotton mill, to keep the mills running."

"Loyal to who?" the Irishman asked, getting red in the face. "Who do you mean loyal to?"

"To the mill owners who offer work," he said.

"A worker has no friend among mill owners," the Irishman said. "The only friend in the world he has ever had is the man who works alongside him. And if he won't strike, he is not loyal to his only friend."

The Yankee was slow to speak, but he was determined in his stand.

"I'm going to work tomorrow, and every day that the mills stay open," he said.

"You're going to scab tomorrow, you mean," the Englishman said.

"Every man among us who helps keep the mills running is a scab," the Irishman said.

The restaurant owner spoke up.

"If the loyal workers don't keep the mills running, I'll be ruined," he said. "I can't run my business when people are striking. I'll be bankrupt inside a month."

"If the traitorous workers keep the mills running, you ought to go bankrupt, and may God speed you on your way," the Irishman said. "If I had my way about it, I'd take just such people as you and shove you into a mill job that pays fifty cents a day. That would wake up whatever is left in you."

"I'm in favor of the fifty-cent workers going on strike," the Yankee said. "But that doesn't affect me any. I'm going to make all I can as long as I can."

"Then how in the world can fifty-cent workers win a strike if all the workers don't back them up?" the Englishman said. "If half the textile workers are out on strike, and half not on strike, the strikers have no more chance of winning than I have of sprouting wings to fly to Heaven on."

The Yankee and the lunchroom owner withdrew from the table.

"If we don't win this strike," the Irishman said, pointing his finger at the Yankee, "one of these days you will come around whining about your fifty-cents-a-day wage. And if we don't win it, it will be because just such people as you kept us from winning it."

"If you saw it like I do," the Yankee said, "you'd keep your job in times like these and put away your savings every week. Anybody who strikes now deserves to suffer."

"And if I saw it like you do," the Irishman said, "I'd hide me shame by jumping in the river. I wouldn't live to be a scab."

CHAPTER XXIII.

WHILE A CITY SLEEPS

At TWO o'clock in the morning a heavy gray fog began rolling in from the Atlantic Ocean, blotting out the harbor. On the foreshore the lights of the city winked out in the fog like candles in a wind. From then until dawn Portland, Maine, was asleep.

The city was asleep, but some of the people were awake.

Along the streets of the waterfront half a dozen all-night lunchstands and rooming-houses were open for business behind fog-clouded windows. From the lamp posts, water dripped noiselessly to the glistening cobblestones.

In a dark doorway a woman huddled on her haunches against the damp night. A shawl over her head was beaded already with moisture. In

139

her hands she clutched a small bundle of pencils with blunt, unsharpened ends.

Across the cobble street darted a black wharf rat, its glistening laminated tail gliding like an eel in its wake.

A clock somewhere in the fog struck three.

A block from the waterfront, down Fore Street from India, a man opened the fog-clouded door of an eating place. Chairs scraped on the floor and a boy stopped playing the slot-machine. The three men in the room watched for bulges under the other man's coat. They soon saw that he carried no gun.

"What do you want?" he was asked.

He laid two nickels on the counter and pointed at the franks. The cook slit open two rolls and dropped them inside.

The man ate one and wrapped the other one in paper and put it into his pocket. As he opened the door, the boy dropped another nickel into the slot-machine. The best he could do was three bars.

Outside on the street the man took out the roll and handed it to a woman who suddenly took form in the fog. She handed him a sack, keeping one for herself. Together they started up the hill towards the brick residences to wait for the trash cans to be set out.

Out of the fog another figure came. He was tall and pale-faced. Coming down Fore Street he looked like a telephone pole in motion. Once he jumped when a rat darted across the street and brushed against his ankle.

In a lighted doorway a woman drowsed in a chair. At the sound of his footsteps she jerked awake and leaned forward to beckon to him with her hand.

"Nice room for a quarter," she said.

He drew away from her.

"What's the matter with you?" she said. "Broke?"

He said nothing.

The woman pulled her coat closer around her and dropped her head into the warmth of her bosom.

Back on India Street the woman with a bundle of pencils in her hand drew the damp shawl tighter around her head. She moved closer into the corner of the doorway, crouched on her haunches for warmth.

Down towards the waterfront a light gleamed through the clouded windows of a room on the street. A man came up the hill and opened the door. An electric buzzer startled the woman in the chair. She jumped to her feet, rubbing her eyes. The man went inside and closed the door.

"A bottle of beer?" the woman asked.

The man said nothing, and she opened the ice-box and took out a bottle.

"Only a dime," she said. "And music goes with it."

The man laid down ten cents. She opened the bottle and turned on the music. The music-box began playing "Cry a Little."

"It's pretty late to be out," the woman said. "We can fix you a bed upstairs."

"Who's we?" the man asked.

"Me and my partner. She's upstairs now."

When the music-box stopped playing, the man got up.

"Buy another bottle," the woman said, "and I'll turn it on again."

The man shook his head and went out into the street.

The woman followed him outside.

"What's the matter with you?" she said. "Broke?"

The man said nothing.

"I can fix you up for fifteen cents," the woman said. "Fifteen cents is cheap for all you'll get."

He turned and left her.

Back on Fore Street, from a dark doorway, a girl ran crying into the night. A dozen feet away she slipped and fell on the hard round cobblestones. Stumbling to her feet, she got up and ran crying into the fog.

Dawn was beginning to break in the east.

CHAPTER XXIV.

WELCOME HOME

WHEN a person has been away from home for three months, and has traveled nearly six thousand miles to return, his pulse quickens at the sight of familiar scenes. Auburn, Maine, is a city of dingy outskirts and dilapidated tenements, but at dusk in a late summer evening the squalor was hard to see.

The summer season was over, the Labor Day crowds had passed into Massachusetts and New York, and the price of gasoline had been reduced four cents a gallon. The State of Maine was settling down among its own people for a long winter.

The diner was located near the Portland highway, and it was a convenient place to stop for a meal. I drove into the parking lot beside the diner.

As soon as I stopped, Charlie came to the window and looked at the car. It was the same old Charlie looking at license plates. The year before he had counted automobiles from every state in the Union, from the Territories, and from all the Canadian Provinces. Now he marked up another customer from the West.

Charlie did not recognize me. He laid out a menu card and wiped off the table.

"How do you like it down East?" Charlie asked.

I glanced up at him, expecting him to recognize me when our eyes met. But Charlie was merely serving another customer with Western license plates on his car.

"I like it all right," I said. "How do you like it?"

Charlie stopped wiping the table and looked at me with a penetrating stare.

"Why, I live here," he said.

Charlie's menu card listed a special dinner for forty cents. It was a T-bone steak with fried potatoes and baked beans.

When it was ready, he brought the plate and placed it on the table.

As soon as he had left, I detected something wrong with the special dinner. The fried potatoes were all right, and so were the beans. The bread and coffee were all right, too.

Once or twice I tried to catch Charlie's eye, but I finally decided to leave the steak alone and make my meal off the other food. Once when he was looking in the other direction, I pitched the T-bone steak out the window.

When I had finished, Charlie came back to the rear of the diner and asked how everything was. I told him it was a fine welcome to Maine.

He looked at the place where the steak had been, and then he looked at me. For a moment I thought that he would realize that I had found him out. Instead, he went back to the other end of the diner, for a glass of water, and looked quickly out the window at the license plates.

He hurried back with the water.

"Did you eat the steak—all of it?" he asked.

"It's gone, isn't it?" I said.

"Where's the bone?" he asked bewildered.

"It's gone, too," I said. "Out in the West where I come from we eat bones and all."

Charlie went for a bowl of toothpicks.

"How was the summer business in Maine this year?" I asked him.

"Oh, fine," he said. "Everybody cleaned up this year. It's been the best year we've had since 1929."

"I guess when there are so many summer people, and in such a hurry, you don't have to bother about what you feed them, do you?"

Charlie looked taken back.

"What do you mean?" he said.

"You know how it is," I said, winking at him.

"Oh, well," Charlie said. "You have to make all you can while the season is here."

"Can't afford to throw a spoiled T-bone into the garbage when the summer people come along every minute or so, eh, Charlie?"

Charlie rushed back to the other end of the diner and punched the lunch-check. When I got up, he handed it to me like a deputy-sheriff presenting an attachment. I gave him the forty cents.

At the door Charlie stopped me.

"Look here a minute," he said. "Haven't I seen

you somewhere before? I know your face, but I can't place you."

"Sure," I said. "I live up the road."

"But you drove up in that Western car," Charlie protested.

"That belongs to a friend of mine," I said. Charlie followed me outside to the car.

"Since you've been away on a trip, it might be a good idea to watch yourself for a few days. When people make a change from one state to another, sometimes it upsets their stomachs."

I got into the car.

"I don't want you to think—" he began.

"Forget it, Charlie," I said. "Just let me know when you get your ice-box cleaned out, and I may drop in again sometime."

III.

DETROIT

CHAPTER I.

THE KINGDOM OF HENRY I

Henry Ford is the father of many things, and he is proud of them all. He smiles from ear to ear, and chuckles deep in his chest, when he is called the father of the automobile industry, the father of Modern Detroit, and the father of seventy thousand men.

Catching Henry Ford in this mellow mood may win for yourself a brand-new Ford sedan, delivered with compliments at your door. But mention of Bloody Monday, the March day in 1932 when five thousand unemployed and hungry Ford workers demanded recognition of his paternity, will prove that Ford is an Indian-giver, and you will find yourself being booted out of the throne-room. Today gardeners tend the flowers that have been planted to cover the scars

151

of that 1932 battlefield, but nonetheless a pall hangs over the banks of River Rouge to mark the scene of death. Ford's police were given orders to shoot down Ford's workers, and neither flowers nor gardens nor time can ever cause men to forget Bloody Monday.

The Ford Motor Company, a closed corporation, owned by Henry Ford and his son, Edsel, produces from four thousand to five thousand motor cars and trucks each twenty-four-hour day. The manufacturing is done at River Rouge in Dearborn, an adjoining suburb of Detroit. The plant occupies 1,096 acres, and normally since 1930 forty thousand workers are employed. Ford's remaining thirty thousand children are bums, beggars, and panhandlers asking for only three cents with which to buy a cup of Michigan Avenue coffee.

After bringing the assembly line to its present high-geared speed, Ford installed in his plant what is perhaps the most thorough spy system in existence. This is known as the multiple service system in the plant, and is ruled over by Harry Bennett. In some departments, for every ten workers employed, there is a serviceman to check, double check, and triple check upon his activities.

A Ford serviceman at River Rouge performs the duties of a stoolpigeon. He may be a uniformed guard, deputized by the city police department; he may be an ex-chain-gang captain, brought up from Georgia or Alabama and shaved until his jowls are the tint of a scalded pig; he may be a scab who, during periods of no strikes, poses as a worker in order to gain confidences; he may be a Ford trade-school graduate who has been well trained in pushing and speeding-up fellow workers.

No nation at war ever perfected such a spy system as the one which honeycombs the River Rouge plant, the city of Dearborn, and the homes of Ford workers. Henry Ford's fear of the worker—the fear that the worker, goaded and speeded-up on the assembly line beyond human endurance, may turn as he once did on Bloody Monday—sends servicemen scouting day and night. Not content with searching dinner pails and clothing for trade union leaflets, workers' newspapers and working-class literature, Ford attempts to segregate workers in near-by districts, such as Dearborn, Garden City, Lincoln Park, and Inkster, where he and his servicemen can keep an active eye on any movement one is likely to make.

If a worker is lucky enough to have escaped the breaking of the DO NOT rules inside the plant, after having obeyed all day the NO SMOKING, NO CHEWING, NO TALKING rules, he must watch his step when he leaves the plant. If he forgets to cross Miller Road by use of the overhead bridge or subway on his way to his street car, he is immediately spotted by a serviceman and finds his job gone forever.

If he is lucky enough to be able to walk the chalk line to his street car, he must then board it and go to his garden and spend several hours planting, weeding, and cultivating. For he has been given to understand that it would be best to sign up for one of Ford's twenty thousand garden plots, and has paid fifty cents for the privilege. However, if he goes home and stretches out on the floor or bed for two hours in order

to regain enough strength to eat supper after
eight hours of hounding, speed-up, and little or
no lunch-hour rest period, he still runs the risk
of losing his job. Because a serviceman, assigned
to spy upon him, may have been to inspect his
garden and found a few weeds in it. Weeds in one
of the forced-labor gardens is one of the thousand deadly and unpardonable Ford sins.

Ford's desire to be known as the father of all
and sundry was prompter of one of his many
famous orders. Investigators from the service department were sent out to gather complete information regarding the attitude of the worker
towards the great father. The report turned in
stated that the father of them all was known to
the workers as "the big boss," "the chief," "the
pusher," "slave-driver," "Mister Ford," and
other less quotable titles. Ford's action was immediate. The order was given that henceforth he
was to be referred to by all workers, both on and
off company property, as "The Old Man." He
had been assured by his council that the term
was both affectionate and respectful, and, more-

over, standardized a situation which was tending to get out of hand.

The stoolpigeons were notified by the service department to report for the blacklist any worker who failed to use the new fatherly address of affection and respect when referring to Mr. Ford personally. Soon afterward the new regulation died a swift death when the reports began coming in that the workers in abiding by the letter of the law had evaded the intended spirit of it by adding a few syllables of their own. Henry I was quite generally being called "Old Man Sonofabitch."

These are the workers once envied throughout the world. Newspapers through their news columns, and many by editorials, helped to spread the misinformation, always supplied by his publicity department, that Ford's workers are the highest paid and enjoy the most ideal working conditions in the automobile industry. When it is announced throughout the nation that Ford has raised the wage scale in his plant, the statement is merely a clever non-paid advertisement. Press associations plaster every newspaper front page in the country with such announcements as that Ford's minimum wage scale has been increased to five, or six, or seven dollars a day. No mention is ever made of the fact that, in order to cover the raise in pay, Ford had instituted a new speed-up on the conveyor and assembly lines, had increased the hourly production schedule, and had laid off enough men in every department to more than save himself money on the new wage scale. This non-paid advertising scheme appears about once every year, and for a decade or longer it has been swallowed by a gullible public from Maine to California.

But not even the workers who retained their jobs were always "the highest paid in the industry." The Ford worker, as a matter of fact, receives a lower scale of pay than do workers in other automobile plants. When Ford was paying a worker on the final assembly line five dollars a day, in the same department in the Hudson plant the worker doing the same operation received six dollars and eighty cents a day, and in the Plymouth plant, seven dollars.

In addition to this, the Ford worker is the victim of the most inhuman system of extracting labor known in any industry. The speed-up system—of which Ford is the proud papa—drives men insane. Others are so wrecked physically that they can never work again. After having invented the speed-up—which was later introduced into cotton mills as the stretch-out—Ford is still the leader. No other motor car manufacturer in America dares drive men as Ford does. He is proud of his man-killing system, and his engineers are constantly improving it to such an extent that, at the present rate of increase in speed, workers will soon be forced to run in order to keep up with their labor. Once there was a time when the Ford workers could stand still and perform their labor; today in many departments they must actually hop, skip, and jump while performing it; tomorrow the workers face the likelihood of being forced to run while bolting frames and tightening nuts. A bedridden wreck of a man, a victim of Ford's speed-up, muttered, "May God rest Henry Ford's soul for his hop-skip-and-jump," while watching from his window the changing of shifts at River Rouge.

For the workers at their jobs there is no time to flex a kink out of a contracted muscle; no time to straighten up your back; no time to get a drink of water; hurry, hurry, hurry; no time to draw your handkerchief to wipe your nose— wipe it on your sleeve or let it run. Some days you will have thirteen minutes in which to eat your lunch and catch your breath and get to the toilets. Take your choice between losing your job and being constipated. The servicemen are holding a stop-watch on you. If you say to the man next to you that it's hot today, the man may be a stool and report you to the blacklist for complaining about working conditions, and the next morning you will find yourself standing in Miller Road with four or five or six thousand other unemployed workers wondering how in the world you got there.

The Ford kingdom embraces not only River Rouge and Dearborn, but the city of Detroit as well. Job-selling agents comb the metropolitan area extracting forty dollars in exchange for the promise of a job at Ford's. By some method employed by them, the hiring office will actually produce a job for you at Ford's. But for some reason or other, it lasts only two or three weeks, and it all has to be done over again, if you have another forty dollars. The forty-dollar turn-over is profitable to everybody concerned, save the worker. Real estate agents have a method of their own. If you will agree to buy a house from certain ones in Dearborn, you can get with your down payment the promise of a job at River Rouge. But somehow it never turns out to be in the worker's favor. At the end of two or three weeks you are fired, you find yourself unable to keep up the payments on your home, and you are back where you started from, after everybody, including somebody in the close vicinity of River Rouge, has taken a cut from your savings. On Michigan Avenue there are automobile dealers who will sell a Ford car, brand-new right off the assembly line, for only fifty dollars down payment. The receipt can be taken to Ford's hiring office, and the flimsy slip of paper works more magic than there is in a whole book of tricks. Strangely enough, when the car has been paid for, the worker stands a grave chance of losing his job at Ford's. And Ford tacks up little cards at River Rouge which say: "We do not require our employees to own Ford cars, but we advise them to do so."

Ford has discontinued the emergency hospital at his plant, and in its place has substituted several first-aid kits and a few nurses to explain how to use them in case of accident. The constant sight of so many injured workers at the plant disturbed his peace of mind.

And so Ford built, not at River Rouge, not in Dearborn, but in Detroit, the Henry Ford Hospital. There the injured worker, instead of receiving medical and surgical treatment from the company that employed him, is forced to pay seven dollars and a half a day after the period allotted him by the state compensation laws has expired. He is not taken to the other city hospitals where the charge is four-fifty a day. When Ford pays his workers six dollars a day for their labor, he charges them seven dollars and a half a day for their injuries.

The only workers' organizations that have made an attempt to demand recognition of workers' rights are, the former Auto Workers' Union and the present Mechanics' Educational Society of America. The A.W.U. had several hundred members at Ford's, and this was accomplished without aid from the American Federation of Labor. The M.E.S.A., on the surface an independent union, has accomplished nothing under its present leadership, and it probably never will accomplish anything for the worker in the automobile industry until the covert influence of the A.F.L. leadership has been removed.

Ford has many good reasons of his own for not allowing workers at River Rouge to organize. Not even company unions, which other automobile manufacturers tolerate, are permissible at Ford's. In the Kingdom of Henry I, the right of labor to bargain collectively has never been taken seriously. Ford laughed when other manufacturers signed the NRA code. One of his principal reasons for not signing it was the provision which would have forced company unions into

River Rouge. There is no power yet strong enough to force him to allow workers to organize for their own benefit. He is the power unto himself.

For isn't he King Henry I?

CHAPTER II.

THE EIGHT-FINGER CITY

The NRA poured millions of dollars into the pockets of automobile manufacturers. Companies that operated during the first quarter of 1933 at losses of hundreds of thousands of dollars were able with the help of the government to speed up production to such an extent that millions were made during the first quarter of 1934, and billions in the 1935 first quarter.

The Briggs Manufacturing Company, a corporation making automobile bodies, operated at a loss of nearly a million during the first three months of 1933. At the end of the corresponding period in 1934 the profit of the company was more than a million and a half dollars. The first quarter profit in the following year was

164

doubled. This was made possible, and legal, by an Administration that rose to power on promises of helping the worker.

The worker, however, paid the profit with his own blood. Under NRA sanction manufacturers were able to speed up production at a rate ranging from ten per cent to twenty-five per cent by requiring workers to increase their output, and at the same time eliminating thousands of workers. The laying off of one worker out of each ten formerly employed, forcing the remaining nine to increase their output anywhere from ten per cent to twenty-five per cent, was the golden road to company profit. In most cases this actually made money for the manufacturer without his having to increase production. The saving accomplished merely by firing one worker out of ten netted him thousands of dollars overnight.

The worker himself was the goat from the start. If he protested against the speed-up, he was fired outright. If he asked for more pay for doing more labor, he was laid off. And if he demanded of the company that he be given the right, as promised under the NRA, to organize a local of his own selection, he was kicked out of the plant, blacklisted, and spied upon. The NRA worked only from one end, and that was the company end.

Under pressure of millions of workers, most motor car manufacturers were eventually forced to recognize the rights of workers to organize, but they did so by means of a convenient NRA loophole which permitted the manufacturer to set up and operate his own company union. The worker has no privilege in a company union. It is merely another department of the plant, and the manufacturer rules it with the same hand that rules throughout his organization. Ford alone in Detroit was able to deny workers the right even to make a show of organizing themselves.

The immediate effect of the NRA in the automobile industry was an overnight toll of life, extracted, as might be expected, from the workers. Departments that received orders to speed up were strewn with the bodies and limbs of men who were being fed to the NRA. No preparation was made to safeguard the worker, and he was slaughtered right and left. Workers arrived at the plants to find their machines geared up to higher speed, with no warning given, and they were unable to adjust themselves overnight to the new tempo. No safety devices were provided in most plants, and even where they were installed, the foremen ordered the men to remove them because they retarded production.

Given an inch, the manufacturers took a mile. The speed-up has never slackened; it is increasing notch by notch every day. A worker finds his machine speeded-up several notches again and again, and the company unions are deaf to demands to stop it.

In the plants of the L. A. Young Spring and Wire Company, where girls are employed on light work at wages of seven and eight dollars a week, the speed-up came recurrently without warning. In the course of a week thirty-six girls lost one or more fingers, and in some cases hands, because of the increased speed of the machines that had been geared to a higher ratio without notice or warning to the workers.

At the Hudson body plant the speed-up increased the production of fenders in one department from six and one-half a man per hour to ten a man per hour. This was made possible by firing ten per cent of the workers in the department and by raising the pay of those remaining one per cent. At Hudson's, new production schedules were posted from day to day, each time with an increase. For every wage increase of one per cent in this plant, the lay-off has been ten per cent, and the production fifteen per cent higher. The NRA was the greatest money-making scheme of the decade. It instructed automobile manufacturers in the art of making profit at the expense of the worker.

The average worker at Hudson's receives between seventeen dollars and eighteen dollars per week.

The Hudson plant, and every other motor products plant in metropolitan Detroit, has taken a toll of fingers, hands, arms, legs, and crushed bodies. The refusal to install safety devices, because they retard production, is general in the district. And where the safeguards are installed, the safety department winks at the fore-

men, then the foremen order them disconnected
as soon as the safety men have left the department. Even fire extinguishers in many plants
have been removed from entire buildings to
make room for new machinery.

In working-class Detroit you are known by
your hands. If you have all your fingers intact,
you are either a non-automobile worker, or a
new worker, or an exceptionally lucky automobile worker. If you have one finger missing,
it serves as an identification device. But when
two fingers have been torn from your hands,
you are an outcast. The hiring departments look
at the state of your hands before they look at
the color of your skin. There is no use in filling
out an application blank for an automobile
plant job if you are eight-fingered. You are done
for. You may as well get out of Detroit and
stay out. The finishing touch has been put on
you for the rest of your life.

At the Dodge plant, speed-up was increased
twenty-five per cent in one season. The machines
in the press work department were increased in
speed without warning, and during the first

hour under the new production schedule, two workers in this one department lost fingers. During the second hour the increased vibration shook loose a motor from the top of a machine and fell, killing the worker operating it. Hour after hour the toll of life and limb increased. Those workers who were able to remain at their machines were forbidden to gather in groups of more than two. The foreman held over them the threat of losing their jobs if they talked about the danger under the new speed-up schedule.

At the Midland Steel plant, where chassis frames are made for Chrysler and other motor cars, the speed-up increased faster than the finished product could be safely removed and stored. Frames piled up ten, fifteen, twenty feet high. Workers were forced to continue at their places regardless of the danger from falling frames. When the first worker was crushed to death by toppling frames, the foreman ordered the men to turn their backs on the stacks of steel. When the second worker was killed, the foreman threatened to fire anyone who looked at the stacks. When the third stack toppled over

and crushed a third worker to death, the foreman fired two men who demanded that something be done to stop the slaughter.

At plant after plant the toll continued under
the sanction of the NRA. At Budd Wheel,
Motor Products, Ford's, Chevrolet, Murray
Body, Kelsey-Hayes Wheel, Briggs Body, Chrysler's, Ternstedt's, Packard's, Dodge, and wherever motor cars are assembled and products
manufactured, the killing speed of the conveyor
and assembly lines and of the presses and drills
turns out hour after hour the eight-fingered men
of Detroit. At the first hint of a strike for better
working conditions, government investigators
swarm into Detroit to devise means and methods
of averting it.

When once a worker has lost the required
number of fingers, he may as well go whistle up
a rain-pipe for an automobile plant job. His
days in that kind of work are over as far as the
companies are concerned. You will find Detroit's eight-fingered men filling gas tanks at
garages, washing dishes in restaurants, and
standing in lines before the employment agen-

cies that ship men out of town. You will see many of them walking up and down Michigan and Woodward avenues, not going anywhere, but hoping something will turn up.

Once you become eight-fingered, you are a marked man in Detroit. Hotels will not hire Negro porters if so much as one finger is missing. Transportation companies inspect the hands of applicants even before handing out application blanks. Store owners shake their heads at job seekers whose fingers are not all there. Work for the eight-fingered narrows down to filling-station jobs and dish washing, and already there is a growing tendency to close these jobs to them. Eighteen or forty, it does not matter what the age may be; if you are eight-fingered, you are done for in Detroit.

Appeals to the A.F.L., to the M.E.S.A., to the company unions are without effect. These boss-ridden organizations have never come to the aid of the rank-and-file worker. The mangling of hands and the crushing of life will only stop when workers succeed in forming their own rank-and-file union. There are no other means of forcing automobile manufacturers to reduce the speed-up and to install, and operate, safety devices that cannot be disconnected by the foremen.

CHAPTER III.

THE SCHOOL OF PROSTITUTION

D<small>ETROIT</small>, the sometime fourth city of America, is a one-track city. It eats, sleeps, and breathes automobiles. For that reason it holds a highly selective grip on labor. Unless a worker is capable of fitting into the specialized groove laid out by the manufacturer, his chances of finding employment in Detroit are next to nothing.

But Detroit, after selecting the workers it condescends to hire, does not stop at that. It rejects, throws out, and submerges those members of the worker's family it does not wish to be held responsible for. The mothers, the children, and the wives are here not considered to be even the necessary impedimenta of the worker; these persons are the trimmings, the shavings, the waste of automobile production.

174

But the manufacturer has not shut them completely from his vision. He has discovered that in the production of light work he can employ girls between the ages of sixteen and twenty at half the wage men receive for the same type of work. For the hundreds of girls employed, there are thousands unemployed, and it is this threat of being replaced that binds a girl to small pay, unhealthy working conditions, and submission to the foremen and bosses. If a girl protests, she has only to look outside the plant window and see hundreds waiting and eager to take her place.

Wages paid girls throughout the city, no matter how highly skilled they may be, will always be found to be half or less than the scale paid male workers. If a girl receives twenty-five cents an hour doing press work stamping on small fittings, investigation shows that men working beside her receive at least twice the pay.

Seven and eight dollar a week wages paid to girls in many cases must support an entire family. In working-class Detroit families there are always unemployed fathers, mothers, brothers, and sisters. The absence of sick benefits drives girls to stay at their jobs when hospital care is needed, because if they remain away on account of sickness one day or six, when they return to the plant, the possibility that they have been replaced is almost a certainty.

Cases of suffering brought about by the failure of manufacturers to provide healthy working conditions can be heard in almost any Detroit working-class family. One is that of a girl employed at an automobile products plant. She was supporting a family of four, and the loss of even one day's pay would have been disastrous. During the thirty-minute lunch-hour period she gave birth to a baby in a washroom, and returned to her machine. She remained at her machine two hours before fainting. When she was carried out of the plant on a stretcher, the foreman forced her to remain long enough to punch her card on the time clock.

The working conditions in all plants where girls are employed are in keeping with the rate of pay. Some plants, notably Hudson's, require girls to eat their lunches in the toilet rooms. Such conditions are not improving; working conditions are becoming more intolerable each year.

Girls who retain their jobs do so with all the odds against them. A day's absence because of sickness is sometimes seized upon by the foreman as an excuse to fire anyone who has ever complained against the speed-up and working conditions.

Outside the automobile plants, the Detroit working-class girl has an even harder life to live. The few sweat-shops absorb only a small percentage of the unemployed; the stores offer little to the masses; there still remain thousands of girls who are forced from their homes with the necessity of making a living. The streets, the parks, and the alleys are the homes of many both day and night.

The one-product city that is pointed to with pride by swivel-chair industrialists has never, neither in boom times nor in depression years, afforded employment to more than one out of every four inhabitants. The father of the working-class family perhaps found employment at one time or another; the mother, the sons, and

the daughters are the by-products whose numbers and economic value have never been tabu-
lated in census charts under the proper head-
ing.

Detroit finds itself with tens of thousands of
young men who have no jobs, and with no prospect of ever finding one under the hit-or-miss system of the automobile industry. These boys and
young men are too old to be returned to school,
even if there were room for them; and they are
not yet old enough to be enrolled in the Over
Forty-Five Club. It was because of these boys
walking the streets day and night that Detroit,
the first city in America to do so, instituted the
police scout car. The cars, containing two heav-
ily armed police cruise the city in hundreds,
keeping eyes on the unemployed and inactive
young men that Detroit does not know what to
do with.

But the city has a constructive policy towards
its thousands of girls between the ages of sixteen and twenty-five who are without homes and
jobs. Detroit again was not caught napping. It
was the first city to place police scout cars on

the streets to dog the heels of boys whose fathers
had moved to the center of the automobile industry from every state in the union to work
at high wages when times were booming. And
so now the city is taking care of the daughters.
The city of Detroit, with the customary graft, is
in the red light business. Girls may ask for and
receive a very insignificant-looking permit that
is used by them as though they were certified
public prostitutes. By encouraging prostitution
in this left-handed manner, the city welfare department finds that it can reduce its relief rolls;
the city health department is blindly coopera-
tive in spirit.

Unlike the State of Michigan, which limits the
number of retail liquor stores in Detroit to
three hundred, the city of Detroit places no
limit on the number of prostitutes it permits.
As a result, from Grosse Pointe to Dearborn,
the city is the province of teen-age girls ringing
door-bells and knocking on office windows just
as any house-to-house sales campaign manager
would have them do. They may be selling neck-
ties, or silk sox, but tucked away somewhere on

their person is likely to be found the all-important certificate signed by a city health department official.

The bursting of Detroit's bubble did not occur overnight, even though a number of never completed office buildings and apartment houses stand today like tombstones in the city's skyline. From 1929 to 1932 the bubble shriveled; the wholesale bank failures early in 1933 put the finishing, explosive touch to Detroit's balloon-like growth. Workers were dispossessed by the thousands; the hundreds of thousands of persons made homeless were workers' families. This accounts, to some extent, for the numbers of girls between the ages of nine and fifteen who are homeless now. Some of them have found their parents; but most of them are moving towards the city's department of prostitution. Any night they can be seen in downtown Detroit, slipping into and out of beer parlors, hovering in the shadows of alleys, and whispering together in the all-night movie houses on Woodward Avenue.

The few pennies they are able to earn are

tossed to them on the floors of beer joints, crap rooms, and vacant buildings. Most of them are too young to be prostitutes with a health department certificate, but in the empty houses and apartment buildings they are taught to circumvent their ages for pennies, nickles, and dimes. In the back-room beer joints they strip off their clothes, go through a few childish motions of dance routine, and reap a fistful of copper money from the floor. In the crap rooms their busking takes the form of any type of entertainment called for.

Hundreds of these homeless girls snatch a few hours of sleep in the ten or fifteen all-night movie houses. Here for fifteen cents they can doze off until daylight, and then make their toilet in the wash rooms. From then until after midnight, the city is their parent, their education, their food.

A broken-up home in Detroit is more than merely a scattered family. Once torn apart in the one-product town, there is little likelihood of the family's ever seeing one another again. Uncertainty of work in the automobile plants drives fathers to another city, to another section of the nation, in search of a job. The mother may become a domestic, if she can find such a position. The sons and daughters drift like chips on Lake Huron. These are the working-class families that left their homes in Tennessee, in Texas, in Kansas, to answer want ads for automobile workers in Detroit. The wages were high, the hours were short; don't be a sucker and remain a hillbilly all your life—On to Detroit!

Under the banner of NRA, automobile manufacturers of Detroit made millions of dollars. Their eyes, as their spokesman, Henry Ford, says in every cooperating newspaper in the land, are on the future. Ford says, "The automobile industry never looked better than it does now. The depression was just a state of mind. It is over for everyone who has changed his state of mind."

The depression, in terms of dollars and cents, is undoubtedly over as far as Ford and other automobile manufacturers are concerned. But the depression, in terms of human lives, has only begun. If Ford can forget the depression, his conscience will not bother him. He will be able to forget that he wrecked a city of a million workers in order to make a profit of two .billion dollars. The name of its founder, Henry Ford, has been inscribed on the cornerstone of The School of Prostitution.

CHAPTER IV.

F . O . B .

MURRAY BODY CORPORATION is incurable in its stealing habits; in fact, the desire to pick the pockets of Murray workers is getting worse. The gyping of five cents has been raised to twenty-five cents and up to four dollars and more. If they succeed further, the workers will owe the company money on pay day. New metal finishers are being hired as students, while old experienced metal finishers are being laid off.

—A Murray Worker.

Two-thirds of the workers in the Plymouth plant have been laid off, and nobody knows when they are coming back—if at all. In the department in which I worked till I was laid off

—the motor assembly—they have greatly increased the speed-up. We used to turn out one hundred and sixty jobs a day, while at present they are turning out two hundred and twenty jobs with less men in the department.

—A Plymouth Worker.

There has been a twenty-five per cent lay off in the Dodge plant, but production has dropped only fifteen per cent. How do they do it? The answer is: More speed-up. They are also pulling the trick of shifting men from one department to another and starting them at beginner's wages.

—A Dodge Worker.

Workers at Budd Wheel are shifted from one department to another and find that their pay has been cut. And if you don't like it, out you go. Women workers have been fired for being absent one day from the job, unable to keep up with the speed-up. One girl had a very serious operation and was fired because she took a day off.

—A Budd Worker.

In the press room at Murray Body where I work, most of us get only about ten dollars to fourteen dollars a week, while a few of the bosses' pets make twenty-six dollars. At the same time men are being hired daily, and we who have been working here four or five months are being sent home due to "shortage of stock." On the midnight shift they put out the lights during lunch hour and make us eat in the dark.

—A Murray Worker.

Three men have been crippled for life within two weeks in Department N-646, Motor Building, at the Ford plant. The most recent case happened about a week ago. A fellow had his foot crushed by falling steel. After going to the first aid and having it dressed, he was forced to continue working. Three days later his foot had to be amputated.

—A Ford Worker.

I am now working only two days a week at the Packard plant. One day the foreman called a bunch of us into the office and asked how many dependents we had. He made a lot of us think we were going to be laid off; then he used this as a means of speeding us up.

—A Packard Worker.

The forty-hour week has finally reached the Hudson company. Now that the company is getting fewer orders, it has decided to abide by the NRA code and put its workers on the forty-hour week. In a couple of weeks we will be on the thirty-five-hour week, then the thirty-hour week, then Bingo!, we'll be lining up again in front of the souplines and welfare relief stations.

—A Hudson Worker.

The Chevrolet plant is filthy. It may be General Motors, but it looks like general decay. No coat racks; half the time you find your coat on the greasy floor being tramped upon. There are no wash rooms, just six wash bowls for six thousand workers, or one wash bowl per one thousand. There are very few men here over thirty-five or forty; mostly young workers between eighteen and twenty-five.

—A Chevrolet Worker.

I am working at the openhearth at Ford's, dismantling junked cars on an average of one hundred and ninety a day, where previously we did one hundred and thirty cars. The bosses are going wild trying to speed up to two hundred and twenty-five cars a day. Two workers must take off all the door handles, hardware inside and out, also all glass, in seven and one-half minutes. A second delay, due to rusty screws and bolts, jams the conveyor line. Before we get through to the inside of the car, the acetylene men are at work blazing away, cutting off drive shafts, motor hangers, steering column, etc. The intense heat within the car drives us crazy. Once a worker had trouble removing glass and found himself surrounded on all sides by torch and sledge men, and he could not get through the doors. He had to break the rear glass and crawl out head first, and was lucky his head was not crushed open with a sledge, because the boss never lets a worker stop at Ford's. After a day's work we are not only tired, but we can't read or concentrate. Our mind does not work. We are becoming more and more worse slaves than the ancient slaves when they had no machinery to work with.

—A Ford Worker.

I am one of the twenty girls recently taken on at Murray Body at thirty cents an hour. The first day we worked, the boss came around and promised one girl a raise if she would be friendly. She turned him down, and at the end of the shift she was fired. He tried again the next day, and the girl told us she had not worked in seven months, and that she would have to take the raise because she was trying to support her family.

—A Murray Worker.

In 1931, set-up men on bullard automatics in the Ford rolling mill took care of four machines and at the same time our wages were one dollar and ten cents per hour. Now, even after the raise, we earn less than sixty-five cents per hour, and must take care of ten machines. In another department, on the bushing jobs, seven men do the work ten men used to do before the recent raise in pay.

—A Ford Worker.

There isn't a day at Midland Steel when someone is not seriously hurt. Not only fingers and hands are cut off, but also feet. Midland Steel does not spend money on safety devices, because it is cheaper to hire new workers at less pay than the old ones who get hurt. I hear that a man was killed on Saturday night, just three nights after a woman was killed. Many young men and girls are being hired for low wages because it keeps our wages down.

—A Midland Steel Worker.

On the motor assembly line in the motor building at Ford's, production used to be a total of one thousand three hundred motors for the day and afternoon shifts. About the middle of March, when the general strike in the automobile industry seemed about to start, production was cut down to nine hundred. For the first time in years we were able to work almost like normal human beings. Just as soon as William Collins and other A. F. of L. officials did their dirty work in having the strike called off, not only were many Ford workers sorely disappointed, but Slavedriving Henry Himself felt overjoyed. As a result, production in our department was stepped up to one thousand four hundred and fifty motors for the two shifts, and two workers out of thirty-seven were laid off.

—A Ford Worker.

I have been employed at Bundy Tubing for about two years, and I firmly believe that it is one of the cheapest motor products plants in Detroit. The day rate is forty cents per hour. One of the worst jobs is the soldering pot. Here the worker inhales chloride fumes all the time he is working. The shop was allegedly under the NRA, but for two months we have been working forty-eight hours a week.

—A Bundy Worker.

On Saturday four workers were injured at the Chrysler plant. This accident was due to the intensive speed-up system in force. For a week and a half, the speed-up on the lines was stepped up daily. On Saturday the line was moving so fast that the men had to work at breakneck speed. The cars were so close together that there was barely room for the men to stand between the cars, and many cars were actually touching, bumper to bumper. One of the cars being tested slipped off the revolving rollers. Since the motor was running, and the clutch was in, it shot forward the moment the wheels touched the floor. It smashed into the cars ahead, pushing all of them forward and pinning four men between the bumpers of the various cars. The men were yelling for help, to stop the line so they could be taken out. There was only one control box on the line, and the foreman would not stop the line because he said he couldn't stop production just for that. The men pinned between the cars were not released until a worker stopped the line himself.

—A Chrysler Worker.

In one department at Ford's, a worker was loading metal parts in an iron box and pulling the box from one machine to another. The foreman brought him another box, three times the size he was using, and told him to use it. After the box was loaded, this worker found he could not even budge it, but the foreman insisted on using the bigger box. The worker then asked the foreman to try and pull the box himself. For this the worker was fired.

—A Ford Worker.

Here is how the settlement put over by the A. F. of L. officials in the Motor Products strike has worked out. In one department there was a gang of five before the strike, who were getting forty cents an hour each for a seven-hour day. This meant two dollars and eighty cents a day per man, or a total of fourteen dollars per day for the gang of five. After the settlement, the men's wages were raised to fifty cents per hour, or three dollars and fifty cents a day per man. But Motor Products laid off one of the five workers in each gang, which means that they are now paying out to the gang the same amount as before, fourteen dollars. The gang of four is speeded up to produce the same amount of work the five men did before the strike.

—A Motor Products Worker.

Thirty per cent of the workers at Ternstedt's were laid off during the past week. At the same time the speed-up was increased. In Plant 5, third floor, in the lock department, the men have been cut to eleven cents an hour. In Plant 5, Department 18, we used to get a guaranteed day rate, if we didn't make the bonus. Now we only get what we make, which usually means a wage cut.

—A Ternstedt Worker.

I am working as a driller in the Chevrolet plant, Department 30, Plant No. 3, gear and axle division. I get fifty-eight cents an hour and work forty-five hours a week. Sometimes we work straight through without any lunch. The worst part of this job is that our hands and fingers get cut and swell up because of the soda that keeps pouring on the drills. Steel chips get into our fingers and they get so sore that we can't make a fist. The men often have to lay off a day or two to allow their hands to heal. The company won't let us wear gloves; they say it interferes with the work, which is the bunk.

—A Chevrolet Worker.

I am an employee in the foundry of the Ford Motor Company, better known as "the mad house." If I had a mule and would curse and drive him as we are cursed and driven, I should be reported to the Humane Society. We are pushed by the slavedrivers for every ounce of energy we have in our bodies. With the latest improved machinery, many men are thrown out of work. Two new machines have been installed in the foundry in the past two weeks; one replacing ten men, the other twenty-five men. This condition does not only apply to "the mad house," but throughout the plant.

—A Ford Worker.

I work at Murray Body, where bodies are

made for Ford. Last week a girl slipped on an oily floor and broke her ankle. The foreman came along just then and said she was stalling, and would not help her. He gave her thirty seconds to get back to her machine. When she tried to stand up, she fell face downward on the hard floor. And when she was carried out on a stretcher, he told her that if she was not back at work the next day, she would be fired. That is how one girl lost her job at Murray's.

—A Murray Worker.

CHAPTER V.

WHERE AMERICA DIED

IT HAS become a crime in Wayne County to show evidence of being an unemployed worker.

Formerly it was permissible for a worker to mount a soap box in Grand Circus Park and shout until he was blue in the face. Today anyone who enters the Park must take a seat on one of the benches; if he stands up, he must keep moving—a startling similarity between the Ford-invented conveyor line and police methods. Plainclothes men mingle with the crowds of unemployed, arresting anyone who speaks to his neighbor while standing.

Police scout cars cruise the city day and night, searching for trouble. As yet no law has been passed forbidding two men to converse on a street corner; but if three men stand on the street and talk, they are liable to arrest, questioning, and a possible jail sentence.

Uniformed and plainclothes police officers patrol the bus stations, railroad terminals, and street car transfer points. If your clothes are a little dusty, if you look hungry, if you haven't shaved since the day before, the order is swift and official. "Move on, and don't come back. We don't want you in Detroit."

Workers over forty-five, who have perhaps worked in the automobile plants for fifteen or twenty years, and who have been discharged under some pretext or another, find themselves the undesirable portion of the population. They have been replaced by younger men and, in many cases, by girls. The companies save money by making the switch. The only excuse needed is some wholly imaginary infraction of rule, and the over-forty-five worker is discharged without benefit of pension. There is no place for him in the industry, when young men can be broken to the speed-up, and when young girls can be hired at half the wage. The worker over

forty-five, who built the automobile industry
with his brains and muscle, is given his walking
papers, no pension, and told to move on, to keep
moving, and not to come back.

At Eloise can be found three thousand work-
ers over forty-five who failed to keep moving.
They remained in Detroit, in Dearborn, in
Lincoln Park, in Inkster.

Eloise is a perfume-sprayed prison that by
any other name would be known as a detention
camp. Formerly it was exclusively the Wayne
County Poor Farm. But times changed. Henry
Ford did not like the thought of having a common, ordinary, poverty-smelling paupers' home
in the vicinity of River Rouge, the Dearborn
Inn, and Greenfield Village. And then, too,
times were not what they were before the speed-
up. Wayne County's insane were increasing in
number. The speed-up was doing something to
workers' minds. Some of them broke down
completely. Others required strait-jackets and
padded cells.

And so Wayne County Poor Farm became
Eloise. The buildings were given false new

fronts, dormitories for visitor-inspection were constructed flush with the Dearborn boulevard. Lilac perfume was sprayed into the corners and cracks. And then the influx of "public guests" began.

The unemployed workers in breadlines in Dearborn were herded into patrol cars and shipped out to Eloise. It was a sorry sight to have breadlines in Ford's city of Dearborn, and so near the Dearborn Inn where invited guests gathered to do business with the Ford Motor Company. Tourists on their way to the antiquities of Greenfield Village to oh and ah over Ford's collection of Nineteenth Century junk were to be spared the sight of seeing a breadline in operation.

King Henry I found it not difficult to do away with breadlines. His cousin, Clyde Ford, mayor of Dearborn and exclusive sales agent for Ford cars in Dearborn, fell in with the plan. No court order was required under such friendly circumstances, and so the unemployed, over forty-five, as fast as they formed in breadlines were whisked out to pretty-smelling Eloise.

And they are there yet. Moreover, they will remain there until they rot and die. A prisoner in Eloise has less chance of ever getting out and going free than a life termer in a Federal penitentiary. In the latter, you may be given a pardon; in Eloise, because of the absence of court records, nobody knows you are there, with the possible exception of Henry Ford, who may need a jogging of his memory occasionally, because it was his order that sent you there. You are already dead as far as the world is concerned.

Visitors at Eloise, if they insist upon it, will be taken to see the cast-off workers. What the visitor sees, is exactly what the warden permits him to see. You will see one floor of one dormitory. Here the beds are covered with snowy, lilac-smelling linen. Rosy-faced men, over forty-five, sit at their desks, work benches, and easels. The beds are placed wide apart, the perfume is intoxicating, and the handiwork being turned out is a thing of beauty.

This is the front for the visitors, but it is only one floor of one dormitory. Behind the front are three thousand workers living in tiers of cots one on top of the other, with no space for chairs, work benches, and tables. The bed covering is no longer white, the men no longer wear white shirts and woolen pants, and they do not respond when you speak to them.

Men who have given their lives to the automobile industry sit and stare at you as if you were from another planet. Nothing to read, nothing to talk about, nothing to do. The scraps of magazines have long since been worn out, the ink has been worn off the printed page. Men sit and stare at blank pages, wondering what was once printed there.

If you can escape the guards long enough, you will overhear what the men talk about. It is their fear of the black bottle. The black bottle is their term for death. An interne will come through the dormitory, looking right and left. Presently he will stop beside a cot and stare at the man upon it. He will push back the man's eyelids and study them for a moment. After that he counts the pulse beat and jams a stethoscope against the chest of the trembling man.

When the interne shakes his head, it has a

paradoxical meaning. When he nods his head, the worker on the cot begins to understand. First he was thrown out of the automobile plants, next out of Detroit and Dearborn, and finally out of Eloise. After Eloise there is nowhere else to go, save into the earth, whose arms are ever ready to receive him.

IV.

SOUTHERN TENANT FARMERS

CHAPTER I.

TENANT FARMERS

FOR four years economic conditions in the South have been as acute as any in the United States, but in the fifth year of the depression conditions have never been so bad. In parts of the South human existence has reached its lowest depths. Children are seen deformed by nature and malnutrition, women in rags beg for pennies, and men are so hungry that many of them eat snakes, cow dung, and clay.

The State of Georgia, one of the largest cotton-producing states, provides no direct relief. Governor Eugene Talmadge, the self-styled "wild-man," the dictator of three million people, who exercises more power than Huey Long, passes along to the Federal government the responsibility the citizens placed upon him—and without coöperation. Talmadge, when prodded, shouts that the state is no relief agency. While he is shouting himself red in the face, he holds one hand behind his back to receive money sent down from Washington to keep alive the men who voted him into power.

Talmadge is riding to greater power on his program of clearing the state of debt. By refusing to furnish food, clothing, or work to one-third of the population he intends to close his present term of office with a surplus in the treasury.

In some sections of the state, particularly in South Georgia and East Georgia, men who are unable to qualify for the meager relief provided by the Government offer their labor—eight, ten, twelve, fourteen hours a day of it—for what they can get. What they can get, one or two days a week, if they are lucky enough to find employment at all, is sometimes twenty-five cents a day. Thirty cents is the average, in this agricultural empire. Exceptional pay is fifty cents a day.

The wage-working tenant farmer, white or

black, at the present time may work one day a week, he may even work ten days a month; or he may, as hundreds do, search fruitlessly day after day, week after week, for half a day's employment. On the other hand, if he happens to be one out of five, he may qualify for relief work and earn five or six dollars a week. Many, however, are forced to live on the minimum, which is three dollars and sixty cents a week. These relief workers are the aristocrats of Southern tenant labor. They earn enough to provide some food for their families.

The real sufferer in the cotton state is the former sharecropper. Sharecropping, once the backbone of the South's agricultural empire, is rapidly giving way to an even more vicious system of labor extraction. The new style is driving the sharecropper away from the fertile land, away from schools for his children, away from contact with civilization. The sharecropper of yesterday is the wage worker of today, the man who peddles his brawn and muscle for twenty-five and thirty cents a day, and who is lucky if he works one day a week during the winter months, and still luckier if he can collect it in cash instead of in cornmeal or old clothes. The sharecropper's place has been taken by the renter, who pays for the rent of the land whether there is anything left for himself or not.

This once-flourishing farming country is now a desolate land. Crop control has reduced the quantity of products without raising the quality. Fewer tenants can find employment. White men are being replaced by cheaper, more tractable Negroes. Land is concentrated in the hands of corporations, banks, and plantation owners, thereby forcing whole sections of the South into domains of absentee landlordism.

There are hundreds of sections in the South where the land has been bled of all fertility and now lies unproductive. It is in many of these sections that tenant farmers have been left stranded with neither mule, plow, food, nor land. In East Georgia is a section starting near the Savannah River with Columbia County and continuing in a southerly direction through McDuffie, Glascock, Jefferson, Richmond, and

Burke counties for a hundred and fifty miles to the Atlantic Ocean. This territory is experiencing the decay that spreads westward through Alabama, Mississippi, and Arkansas. Railroads that contributed to the once healthy growth of the cotton empire are being scrapped, and in their places weeds are growing. Tenant houses, rotted and roofless, are the homes of families hoping that this year, next year, some year soon, will provide food, clothing, and shelter. When the house falls in, the family starts out with their belongings strapped to their backs in search of another home where hope may be continued.

These American people of the cotton country, robbed of their means of livelihood by the downfall of the old systems of farming, are being forced into the swamps, the stony acres, the steep hills, the waste land. The ground they are forced upon will not yield crops. Some of it is soil that will not even grow a good stand of broom sedge.

These hundreds of communities in Georgia, Alabama, Mississippi, and Arkansas exist without roads, and travel is done across creeks without bridges, fields without so much as a cow path.

These are the unknown people of today, the tenant farmer of the South. These are the people who hide their nakedness behind trees when a stranger wanders off the main-traveled roads. Here are the deformed, starved, and diseased children born since 1929. Here are the men who strip leaves off trees, dig roots out of the earth, and snare whatever wild animals they can. These are the people who were forced off the fertile land when sharecropping came to an end. These are the men, women, and children that many urban residents deny exist.

There is hunger in their eyes as well as in their bellies. They grasp for a word of hope. They plead for a word of advice. They have no friend or leader to help them.

The Government relief agencies in many Southern counties are inadequate to help them. Sometimes neither has ever heard of the other.

None of them wishes to kill and steal. He wishes to work, to secure food for his children, medicine for his wife, a shelter over his head. Some have covered the county in search of even a rumor of a job, and there is no means to travel any further. The mule has died of old age or starvation; or the mule was sold by the sheriff of the county to satisfy a judgment. There is no mule on which to ride or with which to work. There is nothing left except the roofless shack and a few pots and pans, and a corn-shuck mattress.

The Federal Government says that nobody starves, but the Federal Government does not know what its left hand does. The relief in these states is administered by local citizens, and in many cases a local citizen is an urban resident who knows the city street but who would be hopelessly lost ten miles from home where there are no highway signs along the creeks and cow paths.

In Georgia Governor Talmadge takes off his coat, snaps his red suspenders, and shouts from every crossroad that the "wild-man" is everybody's friend. If the tenant farmers who are made to suffer because of their Governor's refusal to allow the state to appropriate relief could have their way, it is not unlikely that they would petition the Federal Government to nationalize the State of Georgia.

Under present conditions that is the wisest step that could be taken. Laying aside the possibilities of political upheaval, it would at least give some tenant farmers and their families the opportunity to vary their diet of snakes and cow dung.

CHAPTER II.

THE END OF SHARE-CROPPING

IN THIS Southern agricultural country there is rarely an opportunity for the tenant farmer to find employment in a mill or factory. All he makes is squeezed from the soil. There are days when it rains, and he is forced into idleness; there are days when the soil is too dry, and he is forced to wait until moisture makes the earth tillable again. And there is fall and winter, a long stretch of months, between harvest and planting, when there is little that can be done.

The agricultural worker without land, implements, or stock of his own may enter into an agreement with a landowner to farm a portion of land. The landowner may agree to supply the tenant's needs, including food and clothing, against repayment at harvest time. The tenant becomes a sharecropper.

This agreement varies. In some cases the landowner receives half the crop produced by the tenant and his family; in some cases, when fertilizer has been provided, the landowner takes two-thirds or three-fourths of the crop for his share. Many landowners combine the system of sharecropping with renting, and require the tenant to turn over to him a minimum number of bales of cotton. In any event the landowner stands to come out ahead at the end of the year, but there is no assurance, almost no certainty, that the tenant will. More often the tenant comes out even after a year's labor, and sometimes, if he does not question the landowner's method of keeping books, the tenant finds himself in debt at the end of the harvest season.

In the latter case he has no alternative but to remain and to try to work off his debt during the next year. There are tenants, thousands of them, white and Negro, who have been trying for the past twenty years to work themselves out of debt, and most of them find themselves

going deeper into debt each year. It is easy for
the landowner to juggle accounts when the tenant cannot read or write.

But times have changed. Landowners were
forced to sign crop control agreements under
the Agricultural Adjustment Act. That meant
that the number of acres of cotton they were
allowed to plant were reduced. In reducing the
acreage, the number of bales were cut. The landowner woke up to find that his sharecropper was
gaining on him. The sharecropper was making
as much as the landowner in some cases.

It did not take the landowner long to find a
way to force farming back into the profitable
paths. He told the sharecropper to go shift for
himself. It was then left to the tenant to decide
whether he was going to remain and work under the new system—to become a renter or a day
laborer. The tenant was given the chance to
choose for himself. Thus came to an end the
advances for food, clothing, medicine, tobacco,
and school books.

What there is now of the sharecropping system is mostly confined to tenants with large

families, generally Negro. A man with six, eight, or ten children in his family old enough to work in the fields is given preference over the tenant with only three or four children. A sharecropper with ten fieldhands in his family, generally including his wife and daughters, can raise more cotton for the landowner than a tenant with only his wife to help him.

The Federal Government, since the breakdown of the individual sharecropping method, has gone into the game of sharecropping in the form of subsistence homesteads. An agreement is made with a tenant farmer who wishes to farm but who has no mules, implements, or grown children to help him raise cotton. The land is provided, mules are furnished, and seed and fertilizer are supplied. During the waiting and preparatory seasons several dollars a week are supplied for food, clothing, and stock feed. The worker then has what he has asked for, and may keep them as long as he meets his payments on time. He is once more a sharecropper, nationalized from the crown of his head to the tip of his big toe, but he has a pair of plow-handles to walk between and a mule to talk to. He has no worry on his mind. He is working for the government.

This would be a pretty picture but for the fact that for every tenant who signs such an agreement with the government, there are five tenant farmers who have no such opportunity. They make trips to the county-seat week after week, trying to find out what is holding up their papers. They receive many evasions, traceable either to local politics or to lack of government appropriations. They go back home, wait another week, and return to hear the same story. In Georgia it is called "getting the Talmadge razzberry."

In the meantime, the applicant asks for relief from the local relief office. If it is learned that he has applied for a government homestead, he is warned to stop trying to get two handouts at the same time. Back he goes home, hungry. His family meet him at the door, hungry. They go to bed, hungry.

Twenty miles away, at another county-seat, the food warehouses of the relief agency are overflowing. There is more food on hand than can be given away. People are called up on the telephone and invited to come and get five pounds of cheese. The car is backed out of the garage, and the warehouse is suddenly crowded with people who would like to have five pounds of cheese for the asking. Inside the relief office the phone rings. Somebody working in a store cannot get off from work until six o'clock, and he asks if the warehouse will remain open until he can get away from his job. The warehouse remains open.

Twenty miles away hundreds of persons go to bed hungry. Families of five, ten, fifteen, crowd into quilt-covered corners and try to get a little sleep on empty stomachs. These are the would-be sharecroppers for the government, for absentee landowners, for anybody who would give them a start on the year's crop. In the morning they get up and look at the sky, wondering which way to turn. These are the tenant farmers who once were sharecroppers, in debt, maybe, but sharecroppers with food nevertheless, and who wish to sharecrop again if they can find anybody to sharecrop for. They say the Government plowed them under last year. They laughed at that. It is something to take the mind off an empty stomach. But the laughter is short-lived. They are serious now.

There are cotton mills and fertilizer plants in many sections of the South, but there are no jobs in them for the former sharecropper forced from a farm.

There are small lumber mills along the rivers and creeks, but they already have more labor than they can employ. Road building and repair are done by machine. There is nothing else.

Rabbits that once furnished food for the hungry have been almost completely killed off. There is nothing in sight after that.

CHAPTER III.

GOD-FORSAKEN—MAN-FORSAKEN

A TENANT farmer in the cotton states pays rent for tillable land either in cash or in bales of cotton. If he fails to make enough to do either, the contract with the landowner is broken, and the tenant and his family are likely to be evicted.

In 1934 tenant farmers were unable to purchase the necessary amount of fertilizer, and consequently their cotton crop was far below average. Those with short crops in many cases failed to produce enough cotton to pay their rent.

Their hope now is to secure Government-rented farm land which will enable them to become sharecroppers or renters. That failing, they will be forced into the wage-working class, the most insecure group of agricultural workers in the entire South.

In 1934 a tenant farmer in Jefferson County, Georgia, was unable, because of old-age and illness, to work out his crop. A physician prescribed for his ailment, but the man could not buy the medicine, and no relief agency would supply it. A four-year-old girl in the family died at the end of the year of malnutrition and anemia. The tenant moved several miles away to another farm, but after several weeks the landowner decided that he was too old and ill to work a crop on a rental basis, or on any other basis, and he was evicted.

The household goods were carried to the land-limits and deposited by the side of the road. Another tenant took the goods under shelter, and the landowner gave notice that if they were not removed from his land he would come and burn them.

In the meantime the old man had gone into the swamp, without ax, saw, or hammer, with the intention of felling trees and building a log house for himself and family. After several days he was found in another county.

This tenant farmer had lost his health, and nobody would allow him to work, either on shares, for rental, or for wages. There was no house to shelter his family, there was no food to feed them. The four-year-old daughter had died with her body twisted and knotted by rickets and anemia.

This section in East Georgia is the scene of cases of human want that no relief agency, government, county, state, or private has touched. More than that, it has been publicly denied that the section exists. And yet it is only five miles from U. S. Highway No. 1, and twenty-five miles from the county-seat.

Hundreds of families in the tenant-farmer class live in this strip of America twenty miles wide and a hundred miles long. In other parts of Georgia, and in Alabama, Mississippi and Arkansas there are hundreds of other families in similar communities. There is starvation, deformity, even death, for want of a loaf of bread.

Like the slums of a city, it contains the backwash of America; but unlike the slums of a city, it is unknown and unseen. Officially, on the rolls of the relief offices and on the mind of the Governor of Georgia, it does not exist.

Here is another Jefferson County tenant farmer. He begs to know how he can get a small acreage to farm. He is a young man, not over thirty-five. He is married and has three children. He has been to the county-seat, but each time he has visited the official in charge of government homesteads, he has been told nothing can be done for him for a while. He has worn out his shoes walking there and back.

His children have not enough clothing to wear to school. He will not talk about what they have to eat. Several miles away is a Government adult school, which provides a job for one teacher. The grown men and women who attend the school, learning to read and write, have to leave their children at home because they have no clothes to wear to the district school. The young tenant farmer cannot understand why an adult school is provided when his three children are unable to attend the district school. He thinks it must be the Governor's fault. Governor Talmadge will not coöperate with the Federal Government in supplying the necessities of life, because the Governor has some political ambition up his sleeve. He would like to become President of the United States. He may have to share the White House with Huey Long, but since they are on friendly terms, he is willing to do that if he can only get there.

Across the field is another tenant farmer. He has moved into a cabin recently occupied by a Negro sharecropper who was forced out by the landowner, and the white man had to have shelter for his family. It was the only available dwelling within ten miles and the landowner had promised full coöperation because the new tenant owned a pair of strong mules. No one knew what had become of the Negro family, but it was believed they had moved into an abandoned barn several miles away. The roof had fallen in, but otherwise the building was inhabitable.

Only half a mile in the other direction is a tenant farmer who has set his family up in an abandoned schoolhouse. None of the six persons in the family can read or write. The man sits on the schoolhouse steps wondering where he can find a plow to break the ground for his cotton crop. He has got to pay rent whether or no, and plowing time will soon be at hand.

Up the creek is another tenant farmer. In January and February there is little that can be done in the way of farming, but it is already spring, and the man sits on the ground splitting "splinters," small slabs of fat-pine used for the kindling of fire. There are eleven children helping him, their ages running from one year to seventeen. His wife is in bed, white-faced with pellagra.

Somebody had heard of an organization of some sort that tried to help sharecroppers, renters, and wage-workers, but nobody had been able to find out where the organization was or what could be done about it. The rumor was that sharecroppers, renters, and wage-workers could join it and force the landowners into paying living wages. The organization, presumed to be the Sharecropper's Union, was like a rainbow after a storm, but nobody knew in which direction it could be found.

The man splitting the pine continued to tie the splinters into small bundles, each weighing two or three pounds. Sometimes he was able to get a cent a bundle for them in Augusta—sometimes he could not even give them away. He had sold a load for four dollars several weeks before, but out of that he had spent two dollars for gasoline and oil to run the broken-down truck. He had earned two dollars in two months, and it had kept his family alive. There were six or seven months ahead of him before he could harvest a crop. He did not know how long he would be able to keep his family alive at that rate. He was a tenant farmer without the benefits of a landlord to supply the necessities of life on credit.

The tenant wore an old sweater pinned across his chest, a pair of patched overalls, and some broken shoes. His wife had not been out of bed in eight months. One of his children, a girl of seventeen, had a growth closing over one eye that could be removed by a surgeon. The growth had been there for eight or nine years, and each year it became larger. Soon the girl will lose the sight of one eye when the growth closes over it.

The owner of the land on which the tenant lives is a well-known figure in public life. He comes to the farm occasionally, always once to see that the crop is planted on time, and always once to see that it is harvested on time. Rent is collected at the gin when the cotton is baled.

CHAPTER IV.

HUNGRY PEOPLE

WORKING for a few cents a day, the wage-worker in the cotton country cannot afford to rent a house for the exclusive occupancy of his family. When the rate of pay is twenty-five cents a day, and when half a day's work is common, there is nothing to be done except double up with another family.

For anyone familiar with conditions among Southern tenant farmers, it is not difficult to cite cases that are representative of conditions in tenant-farmer communities from Georgia to Arkansas. These conditions are not typical of the South, but represent thousands of families that have been forced into isolated communities in these states.

One such case was found in a two-room house

occupied by three families of tenant farmers, each family consisting of man and wife and from one to four children each.

While two eighteen-year-old girls from the house were chopping wood from a stump across the road with a plowshare tied to a hickory pole, one of the men came home in the middle of the day. He had finished half a day's work at noon, the first in two weeks' time, and with the pay he bought a pound of salted hogside, and two pounds of corn meal.

The third family refused to share in it, because the wife insisted that her husband would be home with something to eat before night.

In one of the two rooms a six-year-old boy licked the paper bag the meat had been brought in. His legs were scarcely any larger than a medium sized dog's leg, and his belly was as large as that of a 130-pound woman's. Suffering from rickets and anemia, his legs were unable to carry him for more than a dozen steps at a time; suffering from malnutrition, his belly was swollen several times its normal size. His face was bony and white. He was starving to death.

In the other room of the house, without chairs, beds, or tables, a woman lay rolled up in some quilts trying to sleep. On the floor before an open fire lay two babies, neither a year old, sucking the dry teats of a mongrel bitch. A young girl, somewhere between fifteen and twenty, squatted on the corner of the hearth trying to keep warm.

The dog got up and crawled to the hearth. She sat on her haunches before the blazing pine-knots, shivering and whining. After a while the girl spoke to the dog and the animal slunk away from the warmth of the fire and lay again beside the two babies. The infants cuddled against the warmth of the dog's flanks, searching tearfully for the dry teats.

The two girls who had been hacking at the pine stump across the road with a rusty plow-share dragged two sacks of wood across the yard and into the house. Pieces of fat-pine were thrown into the fire and the quick blaze warmed the whole room. The woman in the quilts stopped shivering and began to snore lightly. The girl squatting on the hearth moved back from the intense heat. The dog got up and shook herself and lay down several feet away. The babies crawled crying after her.

In the other room the meat and meal were being baked in a skillet over the open-hearth fire. Five persons crowded around the blaze watching the hoe-cake brown. The boy with rickets ducked under his father's arms and tried to snatch the hoe-cake from the pan. He burned his fingers and his mother rubbed some of the grease from the salted hog-side on them. He stopped crying while he was eating his portion, but as soon as that was gone he began crying again, and he did not stop after that. He said his head hurt him, too.

There was a laborer across the field who earned twenty-five cents a day. This he received from the landowner in the round sum of eight dollars a month. The only trouble was that the landowner more often than not brought him meat and meal instead of cash.

Formerly this eight-dollars-a-month wage-worker had a job on relief, and he received from seven to eight dollars a week. But the FERA told him one day that he was fired, because he had only one arm and could not do a man's full share of work. Cut off from relief and listed as an unemployable, he was forced into the wage-worker class of tenant, and every one of his neighbors said he was lucky to get a full-time job, at twenty-five cents a day. His nine children had to take turns of three in going to school, because there were only enough clothes for three of them to dress at a time.

Back in the room with the two babies there was no food. The husband should have been back the day before, but it was doubtful if he would return before another two or three days.

The girl squatting on the hearth wore a jumper made from flour sacks, and over that a piece of matting for a shawl. A corn sack had been split open at the bottom, and this she wore for a skirt. She was without underwear, stockings, and shoes.

The two girls who were the wood-gatherers sat down on the floor, one on each side of the dog and babies, and warmed themselves before the fire. It kept them busy most of the time getting wood, because the fat-pine stumps burned as if kerosene had been poured over them. They wiped the babies' faces and scolded the dog for moving so often.

There was nothing in that side of the house to eat, and there had been nothing for three days. The dog began to whine again, and tried to get up to go outside and hunt for some food, but the girls would not let her leave the babies. The dog had to keep them until the mother had finished her nap.

The girl on the hearth, raising her corn-sack skirt to let the warmth of the fire fall upon her body, said it ought to be easy to find something to eat if you only knew where to look for it. Her sisters looked at her but said nothing. The girl then asked herself a question. What wouldn't I do for a heaping dish of hog sausage?

When the condition of these families was brought to the attention of county officials, newspaper editors, and leading citizens of the community, the circumstances were indignantly denied. Later, after several investigations had been made and the conditions admitted, the only plan discussed was a sterilization program. Thus it was made plain that the citizenship of the areas will take no steps to remedy the cause of the conditions. Sterilization should be applied to certain individual mental and physical cases, but the thousands of Southern tenant farmers are in an economic condition that demands much more than superficial thought.

CHAPTER V.

THE NEW SLAVERY

Having passed through one of the hardest winters in American history, the Southern tenant farmer today realizes that somebody, somewhere, is trying to squeeze him through the little end of the horn. What he does not yet realize is that his end of the horn is to be a great deal smaller than he had anticipated.

The winter of 1934-35 was a hard-times period in the cotton states of the South, but the winters to come will bring to the majority of tenant farmers an even greater depression. The sharecropper, the renter, and the wage hand of the cotton country are headed for economic slavery.

Whatever benefits a few receive under the present system of cotton production are completely wiped out by the hunger, poverty, and human disintegration of thousands.

The crop control plan as it is practiced in the cotton states of Mississippi, Alabama, Georgia, and elsewhere, penalizes the tenant farmer and enriches the landowner. The tenant has even less now than he ever had before; the landowner has more than ever. Whatever may be said for the plan for limiting production and equalizing income, there is much more to be said concerning the plan in actual every-day practice. The tenant farmer who receives without delay and without discount his parity check from Washington, who receives without deductions his government rental check, and who receives various other forms of relief—this tenant farmer is matched against a hundred others who receive nothing. On paper and on record the crop control program is no doubt marked up in Washington as a great success. In Mississippi, Alabama, and Georgia there are thousands of tenant farmers who have not received one red penny of the money due them.

In certain counties of these three cotton states,

as well as throughout Arkansas, Louisiana, Texas, and other cotton-producing states to the same extent, the parity and rent checks have been placed in the hands of the tenants to whose order they were drawn in Washington. In certain other counties of these states the money has been collected and deposited to the credit of landowners who have neither legal nor moral right to it. It would seem that the fault in such cases lies in the local administration of the crop control act; however, it is difficult to understand how such wide-spread thieving continues month after month, in county after county, without detection in Washington. If there were only a few isolated cases where this is practiced, the condition could be laid to oversight by the supervisors; but throughout these states one comes upon instance after instance where the tenants have signed or made their marks upon mysterious papers as long ago as September 1934 without since receiving any part of the government obligation due them.

The buying power that appears to be a thought uppermost in the mind of the Administration is merely a feeble gesture today in the cotton states because of this misappropriation of money. The individual landowner who collects not only his half of the rental checks from the government, but also collects the tenant's half as well, deposits the money in his bank. The next step is to take over and deposit his tenant's parity check. A hundred such checks in one man's hand makes the buying power of ninety-nine other men equal zero.

The pressure of the landowning class is becoming increasingly acute. This class has almost entirely dissolved the system of farming known as sharecropping. Sharecropping, as it was once practiced, will soon be unknown in the South. What has taken its place is a system of renting which produces more for the landowner and less for the tenant. The renter is obliged to pay a stipulated sum of money. The landowner is certain to receive his income, and if there is anything left over, the tenant is entitled to receive it. Under the sharecropping system the landowner and tenant divided half-and-half, usually, the product of the tenant's toil. Today under the renting system if a tenant agrees to pay $75 rent, for a certain acreage, he pays that $75 whether or not he makes anything more than that amount for his year's labor.

The owner of a plantation who rents his land to a hundred tenants usually goes even further. He sets up his own store, forbids tenants to buy goods elsewhere, forces them to sell their cotton to him, and in the end no actual cash is paid the tenant. If the worker buys several dollars worth of goods at the plantation store, he is charged ten to twelve per cent, or even higher, interest and, at the end of the year, is notified that he is forty, or a hundred dollars in debt, in spite of the fact that he turned two or three bales of cotton over to the plantation owner to sell for him. Such cases, especially among Negro tenants, are common rather than exceptions on certain large plantations.

The white tenant farmer fares even worse than the Negro. Because he usually questions the landowner's bookkeeping methods, and because he sometimes openly rebels against the system of economic slavery, the landowner in many cases has systematically excluded the white tenant from his plantation. Consequently, the white tenant farmer has been forced away from the rich productive soil of the plantations to the stony acres and steep barren hillsides of the uplands. Here he can make practically nothing. Without means of buying fertilizer his land cannot be cultivated profitably. Without credit he is unable to buy farm implements and stock. Here he quickly becomes a liability to himself and to the state and nation. After a few years of this he has become what is sometimes known as a poor white. His children grow up uneducated and diseased; and, finally, broken in health and in spirit, he becomes a member of a vast army of hangers-on.

Unintelligent direction of government relief work is a machine of error. One of the most misguided phases of this machine of error is the ditching operations, which goes under the head of drainage projects. In the face of a rapidly sinking water-level, the semi-arid country is being drained bone-dry. The additional land thus made available for cultivation is a liability, since already there is a surplus of land. There can be no quarrel with efforts to drain the swamps and lowlands, which have already helped to control epidemics of malaria; but the drainage of table-land is another matter.

What actually happens is that this new bone-dry land drains off the surface water which, if left to itself, would supply the underground streams with drinking water. As a result, wells are rapidly going dry. On the surface, the earth dries up and is blown away in dust and sand storms. Unless this squander of water is stopped, the Great American Desert will cross the Mississippi River not without a great deal of haste.

CHAPTER VI.

SOUTHERN BADLANDS

THE State of Mississippi has never been widely known for its prosperous citizenry. If anyone were to take a trip by automobile through the central part of the state, he would find out the reason for its impoverished condition. Here, starting at Forest and traveling northward, lies the answer.

Past Forest, through Carthage, Kosciusko, Ackerman, and beyond, there are hundreds of families of tenant farmers trying desperately, but without hope of success, to make a living from these stony acres and steep hillsides. They have been trying for many years, a long time before 1930, to woo, entreat, beg, curse, and flail a living from this unproductive land. They are the white tenant farmers who have been forced away from the rich river-country lands by plantation owners who breed Negroes for their labor. These white tenant farmers of central Mississippi average from one to three bales of cotton a year, one of which goes for rent. Their mules have become weakened and broken because of lack of food, and consequently the tenant is able to scrape the mere top of the ground with his plow. When enough earth has been scraped together to make a row, the seed is planted. Fertilizer is almost a necessity in this section, but the tenant farmer who can buy any at all is forced to drill it so thinly that its effect is barely more than worth the effort of hauling it from the nearest town.

The income from one of these central Mississippi tenant farms, together with the government rent and parity checks, usually amounts to less than two hundred dollars a year.

On some of these farms are tenants who are well satisfied with their incomes. If they make three bales of cotton, and receive their government checks, they see no reason for wishing more. On other farms are tenants who are unable to make enough to supply their needs, and, even with allotments of food and clothing from the relief offices, they still have less than enough. Men with families of eight or ten children, and whose income is ten dollars a month in wages, cannot begin to live without want. Years of malnutrition and disease have made small children bed-ridden. Tuberculosis can be treated by the county health officer, but there can be no cure without change of climate or living conditions.

The landowning class does not suffer from want. Its income is assured. It has all the Negro labor it needs.

The Negro in Mississippi, who far outnumbers the white man in the state, has fallen into two kinds of circumstances. He in both cases is an exploited slave, the man who was once promised, many years ago, a gray mule and forty acres of land of his own. As far as he is concerned, the war is not over yet.

The Negro is a slave of the large landowner, the plantation holder who has perhaps twenty-five hundred acres of rich river-country land. He has fallen from the comparatively high standards of the sharecropper. Now gradually falling from the renter class, he has become a wage-hand promised ten dollars a month, when he works. He may work three or four months a year—from half an hour before sunrise until half an hour after sunset. If he can collect his ten dollars a month from his plantation boss, he has a lot more than the Negro wage-hand who cannot collect a penny of the money due him.

By renting land from the landowner under the crop control plan, the government has unwittingly given the landowner an opportunity to double his income. If the landowner takes the opportunity offered—and the gradual removal of the tenant from the sharecropper and renter classes to the wage-hand class is ample proof that he does take it—he receives all the money that ordinarily would have been divided among his tenants and himself. Merely by changing terms, the plantation owner is enriched to the extent of several thousand dollars a year. The Negro tenant, doing the same work he has always done, finds that his condition is even worse than it was ten, twenty, fifty years ago.

The Negro is ruled by the white man, and notwithstanding the relief agencies set up to aid him, he is still the victim of the white overlord. On relief projects he works long hours for small pay, while the white man on relief is given the job of bossing him. It is not uncommon to find a gang of workers on such a project composed of fifteen or twenty Negroes, who sweat with pick and shovel, while five or ten white men stand above him bossing and receiving a higher scale of wages.

In the matter of the distribution of food and clothing to the destitute, the Negro again is at the mercy of the whites. Food that is sorted into two classes, the good and the bad, is handed out as "nigger food" and food. If the Negro lives on a plantation, he may find himself among those others of his race who have been forced to pay the landowner store prices for food and clothing that had been sent out by a relief agency for free distribution. If he is unable to pay cash for some of this, he is charged ten or twelve per cent interest.

Mississippi is not alone in such things.

Throughout the cotton states the various prac-
tices of discrimination and theft against the
Negro can be found with startling regularity. In
traveling through some of these areas one comes
upon sections where there is no complaint
against the landowners: in other sections one will
hear of county-wide cases affecting the welfare of
hundreds of Negro families. As a whole, these
conditions have the appearance of a checker-
board design. One county will be black with discrimination and theft, the next county will be
white with relatively few cases.

Instead of buying thousands of acres of tim-
berland for retirement from private ownership, a
practice recently adopted by the government in
the South, what should be bought is this vast
territory of stony acres and steep hillsides in
central Mississippi. By taking over this section
and supplying suitable farm lands elsewhere, the
Government would be performing a greater public service. These tenants would be removed to
other sections of the state, sold land on low
terms, or in exchange for their former farms,
supplied with stock and implements on terms

that could be met, and given a start in life they never had to begin with. Supplies of food and clothing can never be more than temporary makeshifts for a situation that demands foresight into the future.

If some such plan is not put into effect, the result can mean but one thing to Mississippi: the forcing to a still lower level of living of these thousands of American citizens.

CHAPTER VII.

MEN TODAY

ALABAMA has natural resources that make it one of the richest states in the Union. In the northern part it has more potential water-power than any one state could use, in the north-central portion it is underlaid with millions of tons of coal and ore, and in the southern part its land is so fertile that few areas of it require fertilizer. In spite of all this, Alabama's human beings are among the most exploited of any in America.

The fertile areas have been cornered by land-owners whose cotton plantations cover from two to five thousand acres each. To work these acres Alabama excels in its breeding of Negroes. The white tenants have gradually been forced to the hills to till the best they can the unproductive slopes. Where these slopes abound, there is a section of poverty and injustice unknown to the rest of the nation. Even large numbers of the state's own citizens are unaware of these conditions.

In a large section of the state lying east of Birmingham and Montgomery, hundreds of white and Negro tenant farmers are trying to exist under circumstances only a few degrees removed from slavery. The landowners, having in their hands farms that should be turned back into forests, employ every known method of exploiting labor. Tenants are threatened, cheated, and whipped in efforts to extract the last penny of profit. Any effort on the part of the tenant to protest against his treatment is met with warnings to keep his mouth shut. The landowner's riders, covering farms on horseback, keep constant watch over the tenants. Where this method of control is not practiced openly, it is done in other ways. Any stranger passing through this section of the country is likely to be watched closely, if not actually questioned and threatened, by the landowner's riders. A stranger who would stop and sympathize with one of the ten-

ants runs the risk of being escorted to the county
line and left there with the silent but unmistaka-
ble warning not to come back again.

In a state where such methods are employed
by the landowning class, it is not surprising to
come face to face with cases of human want and
suffering brought about by the tenant's failure
to take warning where warning was given. Within
a few miles of the University of Alabama are
areas inhabited by tenant families living on the
ragged edge of life. Here are families without
land trying to live in shacks that are little more
than abandoned lumber piles. Some of them do
not receive any relief at present and never have
received any. Some are heads of families with
six, eight, and ten children, and are employed on
relief projects for three dollars and sixty cents a
week. Some are forced to sell their few remaining possessions in order to keep a roof over their
heads. In one way or another, these tenant farmers are the victims of the landowners. Either
they once rebelled at being cheated out of their
year's labor, or else they had rebelled at the

stealing of their government rental and parity checks.

It would be difficult to estimate the number of children up to ten years of age, both white and colored, who have never attended for a day any kind of educational institution. It is enough to say that in one county (Tuscaloosa) eleven children of this class were found in an hour's time, and what was even more surprising, all of them were white children. Only a state-wide census would reveal the true extent of Alabama's negligence.

The state can be crossed and recrossed, but no matter what portion is visited, instances of the landowner's slave-hold on the tenant comes to light. One plantation in the central part of the state (Dallas County) is farmed by a hundred tenants of the renter class. Several cases on this plantation which were investigated appear to be representative of the tenant-landowner problem.

One Negro tenant had not received his share of the government rent check, nor had he received his parity check. He stated that none of the other tenants, roughly one hundred, had re-

ceived their government checks, even though all
of them had been called several times to the
plantation office and forced to sign papers they
were not allowed to read. Whenever one of the
tenants asked about his government check, the
landowner threatened to whip him if he ever
asked about it again. This particular tenant had
made nine bales of cotton over a three-year period, but had not received a penny from his
work. The plantation owner had deducted $75
rental for each of three years, the tenant had
bought $22.50 in goods at the plantation store
over the same period, but in the spring of 1935
when the tenant asked for his cotton money, the
landowner told him he was $40 in debt and
would have to remain there until he worked himself out of debt. The tenant declared this had
been a yearly happening for the fifteen years he
had worked on the plantation. He began as a
sharecropper, was recently forced to become a
renter, and from all indications will soon be a
wage-hand, due to receive nothing but the doubtful promise of ten dollars a month.

By any fair means of accounting, for the year 1934 this Negro tenant farmer should have received not less than $150 in cash. He was entitled to receive this amount, or more, even after paying $75 rent and the $22.50 store account. On top of that should be added his half-share of the government rent check, and the entire amount of his government parity check. For the year (1934) this would have amounted to about $48, which added to the return from two bales of cotton due him, would be $198. The tenant received nothing, according to his statement, and neither did any of the other hundred tenant farmers on the plantation. To arrive at the landowner's estimated profit, aside from the rent collected from each tenant, which averaged $75 per tenant, multiply $198 by 100, and the estimate would be nearer true than wrong.

Other sections of the state present conditions equally as bad. Within the eastern area of Alabama (Macon County) the tenant farmer who has to some extent escaped from the confines of a plantation system finds himself hounded as well as cheated. Here are instances of tenants working worn-out land who complain to the landlord that they cannot make any more than enough to pay their rent. The landowner's interest in his tenant's welfare stops short when sufficient cotton has been made to pay the rent. When the tenant persists in asking for better land, or credit for stock and fertilizer, the landowner issues his warning. This warning has taken the form of verbal threats, whippings, and killings in eastern Alabama.

The tenant is warned not to discuss with other tenants or with outside persons any matter connected with the landowner's interests. Strangers who might stop and discuss any such matter with the tenant are sometimes followed and trailed by the landowner's riders. If they do not keep going, the riders point out the nearest exit from the county.

A continuation of the tenant system of cotton production means serious trouble for the future. The sharecropping plan was almost universally abandoned when the government stepped into

258 SOME AMERICAN PEOPLE

the agricultural states of the South, not because the government put an end to it, but because landowners saw more money in the renting system. The renting system will not remain long, however. The next step is to be the wage system, which has already worked its way throughout the cotton states because it offers landowners a sure means of making money. The wage system, which means payment for labor from twenty-five cents a day—usually paid in the round sum of ten dollars a month—enables the landowner to secure labor at its cheapest price; and, furthermore, it enables the landowner to gather all of the government rental checks for himself without going through the form of stealing required under the sharecropping and rental systems.

And, with this technicality removed, the landowner is still under no obligation to pay or to allow the tenant to receive anything, because he can warn the tenant against asking for his wages of ten dollars a month, just as he has warned him in the past against asking for his share of the government checks and for a yearly settlement of accounts.

Until the agricultural worker commands his own farm, either as an individual or as a member of a state-allotted farm group, the Southern tenant farmer will continue to be bound hand and foot in economic slavery.

CHAPTER VIII.

FREEDOM FOR THE TEN-ANT FARMER

GEORGIA, like most states, has been so busy telling the world about its natural assets and tricky golf courses that it has neglected to look into the mirror occasionally. Many of its up-and-coming citizens wish the world to know that Georgia is the Empire State of the South; quite a few of its common herd would prefer to have the state pay some attention to its home-folks. Georgia's common herd is its thousands of tenant farmers.

Central Georgia is a fertile land whose center is Macon. Extending in all directions lies land that produces abundantly and yields a handsome profit. If one were able to buy a farm in that section, even a few acres, he should be comforta-ble for life.

But this is not all of Georgia. This is only half of the state. There is a circular rim beginning in the west, passing through the north, and terminating in the east that holds thousands of tenant farmers who cannot find much to brag about. The land is poor and hilly.

Just why the white tenant farmer should be pushed back from the fertile lowlands and be forced to struggle on the clay hills for less than a living is a matter no one has given much attention to yet. As conditions are now, Negroes are welcome wherever the land is fertile, but white tenants are not welcome. A white tenant cannot be so easily defrauded of the fruit of his labor, and consequently he has been pushed back into the gully-washed hills to get along the best he can.

Back on the hillsides the tenant families fell prey to various forms of religious excitement which served to take the place of normal entertainment. Physically, they became abject specimens of humanity. They ate what they could get, usually cornmeal and molasses. As a change many of them began eating the earth, and now

communities of clay-eaters exist almost wholly
on meal, molasses, and clay. Clay-eaters may be
identified by the color and texture of their skin,
which looks and feels like putty.

In many such Georgia communities syphilis is
as common as dandruff. Incest is as prevalent as
marriage in these tenant regions where normal
access to the outside is shut off because of the
inability to travel. They are unable to travel
except on foot, because there are few horses and
mules, and almost no automobiles.

The machine of error whirs throughout Georgia, making the same sound there as it does in all
the cotton states. The plantation system is still
a barbaric method of making money. Some of
the government relief agencies are in incapable,
or rather, in ineffectual hands. Nearly all the or-
gans of public opinion are in reactionary hands.
And the victim of this machine of error is the
tenant farmer. He is too poor, generally, to pay a
poll tax, and hence cannot vote. He cannot read
or write, and the newspapers never receive his
political or economic protest. His charges against
the local administration of relief are thrown out

the window. He is a pretty helpless person, this Georgia tenant farmer of 1935.

There is nothing strange about the appearance on the scene as such men as Huey Long and Eugene Talmadge. By appealing to this majority any man with the necessary instincts can sway the vote of states by promising something, anything. The greater the promise, the larger the vote. Sinking men from the Carolinas to Texas grasp at any straw.

The desire of the landowning class is to keep the tenant in his place. The dominating voice in the matter is that of the local county official who holds office by means of a political machine. He may be the county health officer who refuses to furnish medical aid; he may be the county school superintendent who refuses to establish a school in a tenant community. Their reasons for not providing what elsewhere amount to public necessities are dictated solely by the landowning class. There is nothing that can be done about it until the strangle-hold of the landowner on the tenant farmer has been broken. To break the hold, a union of tenants is necessary.

It is astonishing to find in this Jim Crow state that the economic condition of this class of white tenant is lower than that of the Negro. His standard of living is lower, his education is more limited, and his health is worse. The Negro can be threatened into submission; the white farmer still thinks he should have what he earns, and as a result he is discriminated against.

The local administrators of the FERA and PWA have in many cases been reluctant to recognize these tenant families. Where their eligibility for relief has been forcibly proved to the administrators, the result has been a disgraceful, misguided rule. In many cases rather than lend or give money to a tenant farmer for the rental of land or the purchase of seed or a work animal, the relief has taken the form of mattresses, which can neither be eaten nor made to pull a plow. In other cases a ditch will be dug at the expense of several hundred dollars, draining the earth dry of any chance moisture in this semi-arid state, and which eventually lowers the water-level until wells go dry. Tenant farmers without wells or other water supply can be counted by the hun-

dreds in many Georgia counties. Instead of drill-
ing wells with relief funds, and in spite of this
devastation of the land, the program for the year
is deeper and longer drain ditches.

The landowner-tenant system should not be
permitted to exist. No act of its own is motivated
by any desire save that of profit at the expense
of the physical and moral and economic welfare
of the worker. No other system has yet appeared
on the scene to take its place, and until it does,
the demoralizing spectacle of seeing thousands of
men, women, and children, both black and
white, being cheated and squeezed and crucified
by a profit system that should have no foothold
in modern civilization—until a better system ar-
rives, the present one should make the American
people hang their heads in shame.

The system of agricultural labor that will take
its place in the cotton states is still problemati-
cal. And yet it is difficult to visualize any humane method of cotton production that will
embody the present-day landowner and his plantation system. A unionized wage-scale would be
ideal in theory, for a capitalistic nation, but in

practice it is difficult to imagine any relationship succeeding between the present-day landowner and the worker. A far greater step would be the discarding of the landowner, and the cultivation of the large farm on a collective basis, or else the breaking up of large fertile units of land into small parcels for intensive cultivation by one or two persons.